Terry Oliver Lee

BU$INESS FITS

How to Find
the Right Business
for You!

Business Fits
How to find the right business for you!

First Terry Oliver Lee Publication
May 2013

All Rights Reserved.

Copyright © 2013 by T.O. Lee
Cover © Karen L. Syed
Sassy Gal Enterprises: Publication Consulting

Terry Oliver Lee
www.businessfits.com

Some previously published material has been edited for technical accuracy.

This book is dedicated to all the small farmers and the small town business owners that played a huge part in making this country great. Unfortunately, they are both disappearing.

Introduction

If you expect me to describe to you the perfect business that cannot fail, forget it; there is no such thing. No single business fits every person's goals and talents. No business fits in every geographic area. No business fits every individual's financial resources.

There are many reasons for owning your own business. The most common is just to control your own destiny. Maybe you just want to create a job for yourself. Some of you are just looking for an investment. A few of you want to build a business empire. There are hundreds of other reasons. I hope this book can help you find the right option to meet your individual goals.

Some of you think you already know the direction you want to go and are just looking for help in certain areas. For example, you may want to turn a hobby into a full-time business and are just looking for financing.

You are now tempted to only read the chapters on independent start-up businesses and financing. Please don't make this mistake. Read the entire book. You don't know what you don't know. You may discover that an independent start-up business does not meet your goals.

Starting a business can be frustrating and expensive. I started a business in 1984. I worked out of my home. I had attorneys, accountants, and bank trust officers all working pro bono. I put in some long hours. Once I worked thirty-six hours straight to complete some financial projections.

Late into the hours of a particularly frustrating night, I jotted down my thoughts. The next morning, I typed them up and sent them to *Entrepreneur* magazine. *Entrepreneur* published "An Entrepreneur's Thoughts" in the February 1985 edition.

An Entrepreneur's Thoughts

Being an entrepreneur and being in business for yourself may seem the quick and easy way to fame and fortune, but it can be frustrating. An entrepreneur must have a great deal of tenacity.

I felt quite comfortable starting my entrepreneurial venture. It involved marketing, franchising, and automobiles. I had a BBA and MBA in marketing. I had franchise experience, and I'd been an automobile dealer. I even took the Entrepreneurial Test and scored 93%.

I had an idea that I had played with for more than ten years. It was quite unique, and it took me the first eight years to get the concept to a workable point. I then spent all my spare time for the next two years working on market research and developing the concept. I had a full time job, but often spent 30 to 40 hours per week working on the concept.

At this point I was convinced that the market for my concept was virtually unlimited. I felt it satisfied the largest unfilled consumer need in this country. I was all set. I went to work full-time with the project in order to fund it.

I worked with banks, accountants, venture capitalists, the SBA, and investment companies. No one ever questioned the concept. Typical comments were, "This is fantastic and it will work, *but* it doesn't meet our criteria," or "The economy is just too bad." It was just too unique.

For financial reasons, I had to work out of my home. I find this frustrating because I don't have the office equipment or secretarial help that I am used to having available. There is just too much to do and too little time. I hate lunchtime and nighttime because I can't get a hold of people and have to quit working.

Most frustrating is the attitude of some friends, neighbors, and relatives. To some of them, I am just somebody who is out of a job and doesn't have anything to do all day except sit home and watch soaps on TV This is very frustrating since I have a strong work ethic, and I know that I do more in a day than most of them do in a week.

I have now been full-time on the project for eight months, and it is not off the ground yet. Money is running out. My banker tells me to get a job because I have given it "my best shot." My wife is concerned about money, and that creates more pressure.

Is it time to quit? *No way!* Somebody has to do it, and I'm that person.

And I do know that when the project is a success, people will look at me and talk about how I "hit it lucky."

Terry O. Lee

Chapter 1: Background

I've been involved in small business all my life. I am presently semi-retired and live on Prairie Lake in Northwest Wisconsin with my significant other Marla Madison. I enjoy working around our lake home, and doing a little acting in local community theaters. We enjoy boating and golfing, and play some duplicate bridge.

Marla is a retired Federal Mediator and still does some arbitration work. Marla has written two suspense novels, *She's Not There* and *Relative Malice.*

Marla says I don't "idle well." I always need to be doing something. I still do consulting work with a few clients I choose to work with.

I also decided to write this book. I've learned that people looking for an investment in a business or self-employment usually make their decisions for all the wrong reasons. Hopefully, this book can help some people to find the right opportunities to meet their goals.

◆ ◆ ◆

I grew up on a farm in Iowa. My father was a tenant farmer. From the age of five, when his father died, Dad lived with relatives where he worked for his room and board. He went to school in the winter and worked on the farm the rest of the year. Dad thought he had about a 5th grade education. In spite of his lack of a formal education, he had one of the best math minds I've ever known. He also had great common sense.

Once, when about fourteen years old, Dad and I were working late on the farm. I began complaining, as kids do, and Dad finally had enough of my complaining. He said, "I don't have money to send you to school or start you in farming or business, but you're smart enough to learn how to do a job if you know how to work, and I can teach you how to work." I didn't think too much of the deal at the time, but I later found a lot of truth in what he'd said.

♦ ♦ ♦

I attended college briefly after high school before getting married. We had one child when I decided to go back to college. My dad tried to talk me out of going back, as he couldn't help me financially, and didn't think I could be a student and support a family at the same time. He was half right. He did not help financially.

I usually worked 50 hours per week while I carried a full load in school. I don't recommend this, as it is very hard on marriages or relationships. I ended up with a Bachelor of Business Administration and a Master of Business Administration from the University of Iowa. Go Hawks!

Between degrees I worked for a corporation in the Chicago area until Uncle Sam said, "Come here, boy." This was my only experience being cubby-holed in one department in the corporate world. Good experience, but I never returned to the corporate world.

I got very lucky with my Army career as it was during the height of the Viet Nam conflict, and I didn't see any action. I was in charge of control for a test project to computerize the Army personnel, finance, and medical records. I still hate computers, but they're an essential and necessary evil. They just need to do a job and not become the job.

◆ ◆ ◆

After graduate school, I became a Ford-Mercury dealer using some very innovative financing, which we will talk about later. At twenty-six, I became the youngest individual in Ford's history to hold a franchise in my own name. Because of my youth and unique financing, my approval for the franchise had to be referred to the vice president who had the final say on awarding the franchise. He'd never seen anything like my funding technique; he'd also never seen anybody with the guts to try it, so he decided to award me the franchise. So began Lee Motors, Inc.

Young and naïve, I took over the dealership and tripled sales in all departments within 90 days. This sounds impressive, but you should understand the troubled condition of the business before I bought it. My initial capitalization fell below Ford's guidelines, but I couldn't see where I would need all the money. When I tripled sales, I found out we were in fact grossly undercapitalized.

Sometimes youthful ignorance is good and sometimes it's bad. We consistently performed at 145% of Ford's guide for five years. I'm proud to say Lee Motors received Ford's *Total Excellence in Customer Service Award.*

In addition to being a Ford-Mercury dealer for five years, I spent ten years in the collector car business, and operated an automotive service franchise. I also had experience in the recreational vehicle manufacturing industry, and the open wall home fabrication industry.

My jobs included sales, sales management, marketing, marketing management, and general management. I've started several businesses as an independent and as a franchisee. As a business owner, I've sometimes been a sole proprietor. I have been the Chief Executive Officer, President, and Chairman of the Board. I've also done consulting work in several disciplines and industries.

I have about twenty years' experience in franchising. I have been a franchisee three times. I've also worked for the franchisor in several industries and capacities including; sales, marketing, franchise development, and as a consultant. What does all this mean to you? It means that I am an *old fart* with a lot of experience. I have been well off financially and broke several times in my life. I've done some things right and I've made many mistakes.

We're all unique, but that's no excuse for learning everything the hard way. I hope you can benefit from my experiences. If I can help people like you make the right decisions and avoid some of the mistakes I've made or seen, I'll consider this book a success.

Chapter 2: Get a Job

I previously mentioned, being raised on a farm. My father told me to get a good education and go to work for a big company with security and benefits. Dad considered this the best way to be set for life and retire from that company.

Graduating from high school is what Dad called a good education. The idea of working for a big company was a good option in the 1940s and 1950s. The 1950's probably were one of the greatest times of prosperity for the United States.

◆ ◆ ◆

This career path worked for my brother Bob, who is nineteen years older than I am. After Bob graduated from high school, he received some college education through the Navy pilot training program. After World War II, Bob went to work for Douglas Aircraft in Tulsa. He worked in the plant, represented by the United Auto Workers.

Bob got promoted to management twice and sent back to labor twice. The third time they offered a management position, he refused. The labor contract had been changed so his seniority with labor would stop if he took the management position. Luckily, Bob spent his entire career working in the same plant. He survived the McDonald merger and the takeover by Boeing.

Bob retired at sixty-one with full pension and

benefits. At eighty-three, he told me that he'd received more money from his pension than he'd received in wages for all the years that he worked. We may never see that situation in manufacturing again.

With the changes in business, manufacturing, and unions, nobody joining the work force today should count on being able to retire from the same company. Mergers and acquisitions is big business. If we think about it, the only way mergers make sense and make money is by eliminating costs like duplications in personnel. A lot of people lose their jobs. Unfortunately, the higher you've been promoted in your company, the more vulnerable you are to having your position eliminated.

Many businesses downsize to stay solvent in tough economic times. We see entire plants shut down with production moved to other states or even out of the country. Sometimes companies just go out of business. Many people are put out of work through no fault of their own.

Increased technology and specialization is often good, but job descriptions are changed or eliminated with these progressions in technology. Again, people are out of work due to no fault of their own.

◆ ◆ ◆

The very fact that you are unemployed may make it harder to find a job. Have you ever seen the phrase, "Unemployed need not apply" in a help wanted ad? In my opinion, this seems like a ridiculous qualifier. The fact that someone is unemployed certainly should not disqualify someone for a job.

Unfortunately, some companies use this as a

qualifier even if it is not stated in their job posting. It may not be fair, but be aware this form of discrimination exists.

Human resource departments like to hire people that fit nicely into the hole they need to fill. No round pegs in square holes. For a variety of reasons, most human resource people don't like to hire people who are over qualified for a position. The compensation may be under what they have made historically. The human resource department often feels this can create problems with other employees, or that the new hire won't be happy in the new position so he or she will create problems or continue to look for a new position.

◆ ◆ ◆

Once, when working as a plant manager for a small manufacturing plant in a small Midwest town, I found myself in need of a new office manager. I had an applicant who'd been a bank manager in town. He'd been let go because of a merger. While definitely over qualified, I still felt he was a good prospect. He lived in town and he didn't want to move. He would be taking a cut in pay, but was financially independent because of his past career and family money.

My corporate management didn't consider him the best choice because of being over qualified. Being bull-headed back then, I hired him anyway. He worked out well, and with my recommendation, he took over as my replacement as plant manger when I left the company. Unfortunately, for many unemployed, most human resource people don't think the same way I do.

Sometimes over qualified and/or over educated people are basically unemployable. Have you ever heard that? I hope not, and I hope you never do. For those of you who have, you better start thinking about self-employment.

My sympathies really go out for those of you who have already reached the conclusion that the possibility of getting another comparable job is remote. You're now moving forward to investigate self-employment options, but your spouse is still saying, "Why don't you just get another job?"

Talk to your spouse. Keep them totally informed of the facts and options. Ask him or her to read this book.

Chapter 3: Myths about Starting a Business

I've heard it said that second marriages involving kids are hard because of all the old baggage that's brought into the new relationship. This is also true with business. We've all been told things in our formative years that we tend to accept as true. They may not be true at this time. These *truths* will vary depending on your age and the environment you were raised.

What your parents did for a living will greatly affect these truths or myths. Your perceptions of business will be different if your parents were farmers than if they were small business owners, factory workers, office workers, teachers, government employees, corporate managers, sales people, or in a union trade for example.

You will have different perceptions about business depending on your age. As I mentioned, I am an *old fart* raised on a farm. I will address some of my *truths* and others that I've come across over the years.

> *Starting a business is too risky. A good job is the only real security.*

This may have been true at one time, but we've discussed all the reasons it's no longer true. Many of us have a hard time accepting the new reality. I think it might be harder for women than for men. It's probably natural for women to want security for their families, even if it is based on old *truths* rather than current reality.

◆　◆　◆

There is a movie called *A Great American Tragedy* about a man who had it made until he lost his job in the aerospace industry. The movie stars George Kennedy and Vera Miles. The time period is about 1970, but it's timeless in most ways and worth watching.

Kennedy was highly educated with a very specialized job, and living the good life. When he got laid off, he thought he would quickly get another job. He found there were no jobs for him. It took him a long time to realize this fact and recognize that his life had changed for good. Even after he understood the reality, he went through a period of adjustment.

Kennedy luckily had a wife and family who were very supportive. Unfortunately, this is not always the case.

We don't know how things will work out in the end. Kennedy is finally adjusting to his situation, but maybe making another common mistake for people in this situation. Avoiding these mistakes is why I wrote this book.

> *Start small and grow.*

The opportunity to start a small business and grow it into a large business might have been viable at one time. There are always exceptions, but this is basically a thing of the past today.

A quick look at the changes in any downtown business district will verify the change in retail business. Franchises and chains offer the image, price, and selection the public demands today. We see all kinds of small independent businesses going out of business as the chains and franchises take over specific industries.

Today's consumer demands the selection, price, and attractive image that the chains and franchises offer. Franchisors have learned this and that's why they demand new franchisees start with a minimum investment to attract new customers.

The opportunity to start small and grow is usually not realistic for a variety of reasons. The small start-up usually doesn't have the resources to expand. The owner often works in the business so they don't have the time to *run* the business. Because the owner works in the business they also don't have the time or sometimes the talent to develop a good working business system.

There are still exceptions for specific industries, like the dot-com businesses of a few years ago. Just remember, any success story you hear about is the exception rather than the rule.

> *Banks make business loans.*

Banks do not make business loans. It makes me so sad when I hear people wanting to start their own business say that they have to get their business plan completed so they can go to the bank and get a business loan. They are under the misconception that a bank will make a business loan if the business plan is good enough. Banks do not make loans based on a business plan. I will repeat. Banks do not make business loans based on business plans. No exceptions.

I will probably catch flack for this statement, but most bankers don't even read a business plan and some couldn't evaluate a business plan if they had to make a decision based on that business plan. The only reason a bank asks for a business plan is to make you show you have given it some thought.

The best chance of getting money from a bank based on a business plan is to get one of the bankers to invest in the concept personally. If you're going to the bank with a business plan to get money, your intention better be to get the banker you're meeting with to be an investor personally.

◆ ◆ ◆

Keith Elwick became a friend of mine when I was a Ford-Mercury dealer. Keith always said he'd much rather be lucky than good. There's a lot of truth in that statement. Keith described himself as a farm kid from a sandy farm on the wrong side of the river.

Keith invented the side-fail manure spreader.

None of the implement companies even expressed interest in it except John Deere. They took the prototype to Moline, Illinois for evaluation and decided they weren't interested. Keith decided to manufacture the manure spreader himself.

When Keith started Hawk-Bilt, one of his initial investors was a local banker. The banker invested personally even though he wouldn't give Keith a bank loan. Keith used individual local investors to finance Hawk-Bilt. Besides Keith's banker, his lawyer and several local businesses invested in Hawk-Bilt. We'll talk more about this type of financing later.

Keith later invented the big bale baler. He told me that if he'd had any idea what he was doing when he started, he would have known better than to try it.

> *Build a better mousetrap and the world will beat a path to your door.*

This is a common mistake for inventors and people with manufacturing experience. Historically, the people who invent a product seldom are the ones who make a lot of money from the product.

The people who market the product are usually the ones making most of the money. Without marketing, nobody even knows about the better mousetrap, so how can they buy it?

This is also a common mistake with people offering a service. You may offer the best service in the world, but if nobody knows about your service, you have no customers or clients. Without customers, you have no income.

Consulting businesses are a good example. A consultant may be the best in their field, but if they don't market their services, they'll probably fail. Many consultants feel they must spend a minimum of 50% of their time marketing their business, and only 50% of their time providing a billable service.

A common mistake is stopping marketing activities because business is good. One day they wake up with no clients or business and wonder what happened. Any business plan must schedule marketing and prospecting as part of the daily activities.

> *I will know the right business when I see it.*

How? Will it have flags and banners? Will it have your name on it? Your personal likes and dislikes for a product or service have very little to do with the demand for that product or service.

People often just wait for the "right opportunity" to show up on their doorstep. Opportunity doesn't knock on your door. You're not going to see a building with your name on it as you drive down the street. The business that you don't see, and may fill a need, will not come to mind as you drive down the street.

This kind of thinking is totally based on personal perceptions and emotions. I can't think of a more dangerous approach to selecting a business. The right opportunity isn't going to jump out of your computer screen. It's never going to happen.

A lot of work and investigation is required to even determine if self-employment is right for you. Finding the right business requires research, time, work, and sometimes-professional help.

> *I need to find a business that can't fail.*

As I mentioned in the Introduction, there is no such thing. No single business fits every person's goals and talents. No business fits in every area. No business fits every individual's investment guidelines.

Even if there were a business system that couldn't fail, that business could still fail if the owner doesn't follow the business system. For example, if a business is dependent on direct mail for customers and the owner doesn't send out any direct mail, the business will fail.

The most common error is to think the product or service is so good and in such high demand, the customers will flock to the business. This is hardly ever true. The potential customer may never know the product or service is even available without the right marketing.

A business might be perfect for Joe Blow who is an extrovert and loves talking to people and selling. That same business could be a total disaster and sure to fail for John Doe who is an introvert and hates to sell. Please note, I never mentioned the product or service. It's irrelevant.

> *Why should I pay a franchise fee and continuing royalty for something I can do myself?*

This is a common statement. It might even be a true statement in rare instances, if the individual can in fact "Do it myself." This is not the case more than 99% of the time.

People sometimes think they'll just be giving away profit when they pay royalties to the franchisor. This actually is not the case, because the franchisee gets a lot of help and expertise for those fees.

Business today is complicated and competitive. In my opinion, nobody can be an expert in all areas. The most cost effective way to get this expertise may be a franchise.

A franchise provides a proven business system. The learning curve is greatly reduced. The new franchisee is not reinventing the wheel, which can be very expensive.

> *Do what you know and love and you will be a success.*

This is what is often referred to as *The Entrepreneurial Myth*. In my opinion, it is probably the fourth leading cause of business failure.

I totally agree that people must have a passion for their daily activity. If someone doesn't like what they're doing every day, they will not be happy and they may not be successful.

The problem comes from thinking in terms of having a passion for the product or service and not thinking in terms of daily activities. Having a passion for a job seldom has anything to do with the product or service.

◆ ◆ ◆

I once had a client that we'll call Jim. Jim had loved bicycling. He went to work for a bicycle store, and worked for the store for seventeen years. He finally became so unhappy with his job that he quit with no job or business lined up. I never recommend doing this.

Jim then started to look at his options. His current hobby was horses and riding. One of his neighbors suggested making a business out of his love of horses, but Jim was smarter than that. He knew he didn't want to ruin another hobby by turning it into work.

◆ ◆ ◆

I would recommend reading *The E-Myth Revisited* by Michael E. Gerber to learn more about the entrepreneurial myth. He gives some great examples of running the business vs. working in the business.

One of his examples is a woman who loves to bake pies. She naturally starts a business making and selling pies. She has to quit baking pies herself in order to have the business survive. She has to let someone else bake the pies so she can devote her time to running the business and developing a complete business system.

Chapter 4: Why Own Your Own Business?

There are a lot of advantages to owning your own business. You control your own destiny. You have the opportunity to control the amount of money you make. You control the hours you work. You can build equity in your business, which you can later sell, or leave to your family. You may better control when you will be able to retire. You may have the opportunity to be semi-retired and less active in the business at some point in the future and milk the profits. Unfortunately, owning your own business is not a get rich quick deal, except for rare instances.

The down side is that owning your own business is a lot of work. Most business owners work more hours and harder than they ever did as an employee, and often for less income than they received as an employee. The investment in the business is your money and very personal. It's not some corporation's money that's impersonal to you and your family. This makes starting your own business very scary.

Why do people want to own their own business? Here are some of the most common statements I hear:

- ➤ I'm tired of working for nothing.
- ➤ I can't stand my boss.
- ➤ I want to control my own destiny.

- I think I can make more money on my own.

- I want to control my own hours.

- I may get laid off.

- I don't know if I will have a job due to merger.

- I've been transferred and don't want to move.

- I'm tired of making money for someone else.

- I'm sick of traveling.

- I'm sick of the politics at work.

- I'm just burned out. I have to make a change.

Everybody has their own reasons for wanting to own their own business. Make sure your reasons are real and not just perceived. I'd like to address the first two reasons listed.

I'm tired of working for nothing.

I had some friends years ago who were both high school teachers in the small town where I had the car dealership. They were very secure in their jobs. They lived well. They belonged to the country club and had the summer off to play golf.

They felt that they were underpaid as teachers. They quit their teaching jobs and bought a hardware store in another state. They worked more hours per week than when they were teachers. They worked seven days a week, and no longer had the summer off to play golf.

The worst part is that they went bankrupt in a few

years. Luckily, they still had their teaching certificates so they could get new teaching jobs. Was their perception of working for nothing real or just perceived?

I can't stand my boss.

I hear this one a lot. I would caution people to carefully evaluate the situation and make sure it is a problem that is not just perceived and cannot be resolved.

I once was general manager for a privately owned business. The owner of the business worked in the business except for the winter months when he went south. I loved it when he went south because when he came to work every day, he drove me crazy.

The owner hired a consulting firm to see where we could improve the business. Three consultants came in to evaluate the business. After three weeks, the lead consultant asked to speak to me in private. We went into my office and he closed the door, which I hardly ever did.

He told me I had one problem, the owner in the corner office. He stated that the business had grown and changed beyond where the owner could manage it. The consultant told me I was more than capable of running the business, but I had to find some way to keep the owner busy and away from the daily operations. This was a real problem.

◆　◆　◆

I have seen estimates that as high as 75% of all people dream of owning their own business. Yet as few as 5% ever make this dream a reality. Why?

When I became a Ford-Mercury dealer, the name of the business was Lee Motors, Inc. It was a real ego trip to have my name on the sign, and to call myself a car dealer. The problem is you can't eat the name on the door. You still have to make money.

Chapter 5: How Do You Make Money?

What is the first question everyone asks about owing his or her own business? "How much money can I make?" We better determine how you can make money. In order to make money, at least one of four things must be present or happen.

1. You must have a special skill or talent.

2. You must have money to invest.

3. You must have employees.

4. You must sell.

5. Some combination of the first four.

1. You may have a special skill or talent.

If you have a special skill or talent, you may already be self-employed to some extent. Attorneys may charge several hundred dollars per hour for their services. Attorneys also have staff or employees in most cases.

Medical surgeons charge thousands of dollars for their services. These are some of the first things we think of when we think of people with special services.

There are other special skills and services that command high fees. Realtors, medical doctors, dentists, veterinarians, land surveyors, lobbyists, and some consultants are a few that come to mind. All of these can have profitable businesses if they have enough clients.

Realtors are an excellent example. I have a friend who is a Realtor. So is his wife. Between the two of them, they make about $600,000 per year. This sounds good, but you must remember that most people that go into real estate never make a living.

One profession I was unaware of until recent years is an arbitrator. An arbitrator may command substantial fees, but as with many professions, it is difficult to become an arbitrator. For example, if you now are a Commissioner for the Federal Mediation and Conciliation Service, you could attend their arbitration school and work as an independent arbitrator after retirement. Not an option for most people.

The problem with most things that command a high fee is that they usually require a lot of expensive education and/or special training. If you have this training or are in a job that prepares you for these special high dollar services, you are probably already aware of these opportunities. Since this is not an option for most of us, let's move on to the other three options.

2.   *You must have money to invest.*

If you have enough money, you can invest it wisely in a business and make money. You may or may not want to be involved in the business on a daily basis. Some people are simply looking for a good investment. Some people may want to stay in their present job and invest in a business that can replace the income from their job at some point in the future.

The problem with being an inactive owner of a business is that you must have someone to run it who you can totally trust, and/or have a business system that is so tight that you can be comfortable as an absentee owner.

If you do not have someone you can totally trust, you better have a proven business system. This will probably mean finding a franchise that fits your goals as an absentee owner.

3.   *You must have employees.*

If you have enough employees working for you, and those employees are efficient in their jobs, you should make money from each employee's efforts. Please note the big *If* is that the employees must be efficient and contributing to the productivity of the company.

The type of employee will also vary. A skilled professional should, and in most cases will, require less supervision than an unskilled employee making minimum wage. Maybe your employees will belong to a union that you will need to deal with.

One of the most successful food franchises in this country will have over fifty employees. It will also have over a 300% turn in employees every year. This franchise has an excellent business system to recruit, train, schedule, and manage this number of employees. There are people who love this business model, but it would not be a first choice for me.

You must be able to manage people to make money from a business model that is dependent on employees. A good business system with job descriptions is also essential.

4.   *You must sell.*

People who can sell have more business options available to them. People who can't sell had better select a business model where the marketing is not dependent on personal sales. It may be a business model where the customer comes to them for the product or service.

I've had customers say that they didn't like to sell, but could if they really believed in the product or service. Don't fall into this trap. Selling is selling. I've had clients who were successful in direct sales jobs because of a good work ethic and pure tenacity. The problem is they weren't happy.

Don't get me wrong. I'm not saying there are businesses with no sales or marketing. Every business needs marketing. Sales and marketing are so important that a chapter will be devoted to each.

5.   *Some combination of the four.*

Most businesses involve all four of the above to some degree. All require some amount of investment. A large investment does not guarantee success, but being under-capitalized does greatly reduce the chance of being successful.

Most businesses require some employees, even if

only as a support function. The number and type of employees will vary greatly. Make sure you like to manage employees.

◆　◆　◆

Some people think they can start a business that can compete and make money because they have a better idea, or a better product, or better service, or better price, or better people. Don't kid yourself. Business does not work this way. Companies that have established market share tend to retain that market share.

You may actually have a better idea, product, or product, but you have to make your potential customers aware of the better product or service. The problem is that your established competition can copy your product or service and your competition already has a customer base to introduce the new idea.

If you think you can compete because you can recruit and train better people, you are again kidding yourself. Your competitors already have trained people so you're already behind. Most people will choose to go to work for an established company over a new company, unless there is some reason to go with the new company. Some *hook* is needed for getting good people and this is hard to sell.

When I hear some of the terms used in business today I have to laugh. One I really like is, "I'll hit the ground running." This implies that someone is going into a new situation and knows everything they need to know about the situation. What a joke.

Another saying I like is, "We or I will be giving 110%." They may be saying 150% or more, but the actual percentage stated can never be over 100% by definition. Again, this is a joke. Mathematically no one can give more than 100% and even giving 100% is totally unrealistic. Scientists say we actually only use a small percentage of our brain. Making a greater effort with no change or system is just the idle talk of a loser.

Chapter 6: Why do businesses fail?

In my opinion, the number one reason businesses, and especially new businesses fail is under-capitalization. If you're starting a business from scratch everything takes longer and costs more than you expect.

Even if you're buying an existing business, there will be many expenses you underestimate or can't anticipate.

◆　◆　◆

As I previously mentioned, I was a Ford-Mercury dealer at an early age. We started with less capital than Ford Motor Co. recommended. I thought we had more than enough capital. I couldn't see where we would use all the capitalization we'd put into Lee Motors, Inc.

We were quite successful early. I ordered so many new cars and trucks for inventory that my Ford and Mercury representatives recommended I cut back my orders. We tripled sales in all departments in the first 90 days.

Great, right? Wrong. As we had more new car inventory, we now exceeded our new vehicle floorplan financing. Floorplan financing for car dealers is continually revolving. As new inventory arrives at the dealership, the financial institution providing the floorplan financing receives a sight draft for those vehicles. We were financing our new inventory with a local bank.

Every bank has a limit of how much they can loan any one customer based on their deposits. The State or Federal Government, depending on the bank's charter, sets this lending limit. We had an approved line of credit for our new vehicle floorplan that was the maximum amount the bank could lend to a single customer.

When new cars were shipped from the factory, the shipping time was estimated and our bank received sight drafts for the vehicles on the date of the scheduled delivery. When we didn't have floorplan financing available for the new car and truck inventory, we had to pay for that inventory in other ways. I can remember the bank calling to say they had received "X" dollars in sight drafts, and we were over line and over drawn. Not a good feeling.

As we sold more new vehicles, we had more used vehicle trades. We didn't floorplan our used vehicles. This meant we owned our entire used vehicle inventory. This ate up large additional amounts of working capital.

Everything continued to mushroom as we did more and more business. More new vehicles arrived. We had more new vehicle sales. We had more trades. We had more commissions and on and on. We used more and more capital.

We soon ran out of money. Luckily, I had silent business partners with deep pockets. We'll talk more about this in the Creative Financing chapter. These silent business partners were financially very solvent with bank connections in larger towns. We were able to get the additional capital we needed with signature notes from these larger banks.

If additional capital had not been available, Lee Motors might have been out of business in 90 to 120 days. The cause would have been doing too much business, not too little.

◆ ◆ ◆

The second leading cause of business failure, in my opinion, is the lack of a successful or proven business system. People start or buy a business with no plan. They often think they're going to learn as they go. Think again. It doesn't work that way.

Financial projections are just one part of the business plan or system. Adequate capital is another part. What is your product or service? Who are your customers? Who are your suppliers? What will you need in the way of facilities? What will you need for employees? How will you compensate them? What are their job descriptions? What is your job description? Will you incorporate your business, and if so, what type of corporation. What insurance will you need?

How will you market your product or service? Marketing or lack of marketing is a leading cause of business failure and an essential part of the business model. Remember the "Build a Better Mousetrap" myth. You have to market that mousetrap. There's a lot involved and you'll probably need expert advice in several areas of marketing. Marketing is so important that the next chapter will start to address it in detail.

◆ ◆ ◆

Poor management is the third leading cause of business failure, in my opinion. Every business must have marketing and management. A business can have the best business system in the industry, but if management doesn't implement the system, it does no good.

New business owners often fail to give marketing and management much thought. They think the need for their product or service is so great the customer will find them. They also may get too involved with the day-to-day operations to run the business.

◆ ◆ ◆

I knew a small group of employees who bought out the owner of the company where they worked. This was an established company, an industry leader, had a great reputation, and had made large profits for the last six years.

They'd gone behind the general manager's back with the buyout. They thought they could run it themselves. The general manager had to go. They could save his salary and bonuses.

Unfortunately, the general manager was part of the reason the business had made the large profits. A friend of one of the new owners made the following comment. "They don't know enough about management to know they don't know anything about managing the business."

Unfortunately, the profits didn't continue without the general manager. Yes, I was that general manager, and sometime after I left, I inquired about the business. Someone told me, "I think they are burning the furniture to stay warm."

If you don't have management experience, you may need to hire someone. This is essential and not a wasted expense. Another option is a very tight business system that can guide you.

The entrepreneurial myth we discussed earlier can be a major factor in the lack of management. Don't make the mistake of getting too involved in the technical part of the business and forget to manage the business.

There is an old joke that describes the problem. "I am too busy fighting alligators to remember my objective is to drain the swamp." Cute, but it describes the problem of getting too involved working *in* the business to *run* the business.

◆ ◆ ◆

If I had an ASE (Automotive Service Excellence) Certified Automotive Technician come to me looking for a franchise or business, I would probably not recommend he look at any of the many automotive service franchises. The reason is, I want him to *run* the business and not *work in* the business.

The fact that he's a well-qualified automobile mechanic might mean that he'll try to do the work himself. He might be in the back stall *wrenching* when he should be up front in the office running the business. This can often be a cause of failure.

◆ ◆ ◆

I once had a client validate a computer software service franchise. After talking to about five franchisees, he reported back to me. All were doing well, but one was doing extremely well. I asked him why. I knew the answer, but he needed to find it himself.

He said he would find out. When he reported back, he discovered that the owner of the business doing the best had very little computer knowledge herself. As a result, she followed the system provided to her by the franchisor. She managed and promoted the business. She did not try to do the actual work herself.

◆　◆　◆

There are a lot of other factors that contribute to a business failure. One of the major reasons is divorce. A divorce can mean dividing assets, which may mean putting the business in a position of under-capitalization. The business may have to be liquidated.

The wrong location can lead to failure. We will talk more about location in a later chapter.

The market may have changed. The competition may have changed. The consumer's wants and needs may have changed. Every product or service has some life cycle. We will talk more about this in the chapter on market research.

We see franchise businesses fail as well as independent businesses. I feel the most common reason for a franchise business failing is divorce.

A husband and wife that were my clients found a franchise opportunity that seemed to be a perfect fit for their goals. Their initial reaction was that they wanted nothing to do with this industry, but they trusted me enough to validate the franchise and collect the data. They were awarded franchises for three locations.

The first location did very well. The lease for the second location had been signed when the wife decided she wanted a divorce. The business now had to be sold as part of the divorce settlement. Divorce can be a major cause of business failure.

One of the most successful realtors and real estate developers I've ever known got involved with his secretary. This led to a divorce, and he ended up losing everything. The last I heard of him, he worked as a limo driver in another state.

I'm certainly not the person to guide someone in their personal life, but please be aware of the potential problems your personal life can make for your business. If I discover a potential client has personal problems or problems with their marriage, I advise them to resolve those problems before we start investigating self-employment options.

◆ ◆ ◆

The second reason for a franchise business failing is the franchisee not following the business system. This one puzzles me. Why would someone pay good money for a proven system and then not follow that system?

Some factors that can cause a business to fail may have little to do with the actual business. Some may have more to do with the owner's personal problems. Some people can't handle success. I see people take up many bad habits including drinking, carousing, and gambling once they have more money and time. This will bring down most businesses.

Chapter 7: Marketing

Marketing is essential to every business. With rare exceptions, no business will survive without marketing. A company may offer the best value product or service in their industry, but without marketing that company will not survive.

If you look at the history of almost any product or service, you'll discover the individual or company that invents or develops a product or service is seldom who reaps the largest profits from that product or service. The one who typically makes the largest profit is the company that successfully markets the product or service. Inventors take heed.

◆ ◆ ◆

There are many definitions of marketing. Some are brief and some are involved. The definition that has evolved for me over the years is as follows:

> *Marketing is a total system of interacting business activities designed to plan, price, promote, and deliver want satisfying goods and services to present and potential customers.*

This definition for marketing pretty much includes all aspects of business except the actual manufacturing of the product. In some cases, it might even extend to the people working in the manufacturing process.

Probably the most important part of this definition is that marketing is "a total system of interacting business activities." When we think of marketing, it's natural to think of sales and advertising. Sales alone cannot be a successful marketing plan. Advertising alone cannot be a successful marketing plan. Sales and advertising alone cannot be a successful marketing plan.

What activities are included in this total system of business activities? In addition to sales and advertising, we must also include market research, product development, product management, pricing, name, logo, image, location, signage, facilities, promotion, customer service, and more. That sounds simple, or does it?

◆ ◆ ◆

This book cannot and will not attempt to cover everything involved with marketing. We will try to touch on a few aspects, including market research, product development, product management, pricing, name, logo, image, advertising, promotion, sales, and distribution channels.

I've worked with a lot of people over the years that think marketing is simple or easy. As I mentioned, I have a Bachelor of Business Administration with a major in marketing and a Master of Business Administration with a major in marketing, and I've worked in some area of marketing my entire working career. As a result, I've learned that I don't know much about marketing.

Anyone that thinks marketing is simple or easy

really doesn't have a clue what he or she is doing, in my opinion. It's very hard to measure the return on various marketing methods and expenditures. The market is always changing, so any test market is geographic and time sensitive. This makes it impossible to duplicate and test.

◆ ◆ ◆

As I've been working on this book, I've been reading and re-reading several books on marketing. I would recommend anyone in business, or thinking of starting a business, start by reading *Marketing War-Fare* by Al Ries and Jack Trout.

This book has been around for years, but is still relevant today. *Marketing War-Fare* compares marketing to actual tactics of war. These tactics are defensive, offensive, flanking, and guerrilla. I think an understanding of these different tactics is essential to formulating a marketing strategy that fits your individual company.

Most of you will own small companies that especially have a need for guerrilla marketing. There are a lot of books on guerrilla marketing. Most are available on Amazon. The book *Guerrilla Marketing* by Jay Conrad Levinson is a good place to start. Mr. Levinson uses the following definition for marketing: "Marketing is every bit of contact your company has with anyone in the outside world."

Marketing will also extend to all the individuals within your company. Your own employees may affect the image and perception of your product in the outside world.

As you consider a marketing strategy, remember

to include your existing customers. It's natural to think of marketing as a means of getting new customers, but it's probably even more important to market to your existing customers. Remember, my definition stated, "present and potential customers." Building customer loyalty will generate additional sales.

An important part of marketing is making your customer happy with the decision to do business with you after they've made that decision. Advertising, customer service, and almost all aspects of marketing can help build customer loyalty.

I once did a college paper called "Cognitive Dissidence after the Automobile Purchase." I noted that people often read and watched more ads for the vehicle they'd bought after the sale than before. They were obviously trying to make themselves comfortable with the decision they'd already made.

Did you ever notice how many cars of a certain make and model you see on the road after you've bought one just like it? They were there before. Are you subconsciously justifying the decision to buy that you have already made?

◆   ◆   ◆

I have to address one of my major pet peeves in marketing and business today. That's the use of acronyms. Acronyms have no place in marketing in my opinion.

Acronyms may be acceptable within an industry or company to save time, although I even question this. It may promote a bad habit. Some fields, like medicine and government, have gotten ridiculous in their use of acronyms, in my opinion. Their overuse creates confusion and misunderstandings.

Let me give you an example. I once did some consulting work for a franchisor, and as I reviewed their marketing materials, I kept seeing the acronym "PC." At that time, I assumed the "PC" referred to a personal computer.

The use of the "PC" acronym made no sense. When I asked, I found out "PC" actually was an acronym for a technical term unique to that industry. It had nothing to do with a personal computer.

Unfortunately, prospects from outside the industry were thinking personal computer when they saw or heard the acronym "PC," and didn't understand the materials or presentation. The prospect might think the materials using the "PC" made no sense and just blow it off. If the prospect didn't understand, they wouldn't be likely to ask a question that might sound stupid.

The inappropriate use of a misunderstood acronym made the marketing materials almost worthless. The materials had to be redone, eliminating the use of the acronym. Many prospects had already been lost because they didn't understand what the marketing materials were trying to say.

◆　◆　◆

As you are putting together your marketing plan, remember, you must show the customer benefits as well as features. The benefits of a specific feature may not be immediately obvious to the customer. Show the customer the benefits of doing business with you.

"Sell the sizzle, not the steak," is a popular saying in marketing. Sell the benefits, and appeal to an individual's emotions.

It's true that you need to show benefits for your product or service, but don't go too far. Personally, I want a nice tasty and juicy steak cooked to my liking. I don't really care if it sizzled when cooked.

As an old Iowa farm boy, I know that corn-fed beef is most likely to give me the juicy flavorful steak I like. Corn-fed beef is a feature that gives the benefit of a juice flavorful steak. Some restaurants do advertise, "Corn-fed beef."

A popular advertisement now is Angus beef. It seems to appeal to people who don't know much about beef. I could care less if the beef is from an Angus or a Hereford. I do care if it's corn-fed.

◆ ◆ ◆

People are left-brain or right-brain dominant. Left-brain people are more likely to respond to logic and statistics. Right-brain people are more likely to respond to emotional appeals. Your customers and potential customers include both left-brain and right-brain people, so remember to market to both.

Also remember that people are not totally left or right brain dominant. Over the years, I've seen many people make decisions totally on emotion and then try to justify their decision by gathering facts and data. This is true of people with both left and right brain dominance.

Remember, the decision to do business with you is different for each customer. Your marketing should present facts, features, benefits, and make an emotional appeal. Make it as easy as possible for your customer to decide to do business with you.

I'll give you a few examples of major marketing

tools. Please don't think this will be all-inclusive. I'll just be touching the basics. I'll also give you several examples from my past experience. I'm not necessarily recommending them for your business. They may or may not be relevant. The examples are simply to get you thinking.

As you're putting together a marketing plan, remember, it is most likely that any good plan will use a variety of marketing tools. Newspaper advertising or a good brochure will not do the job alone.

For example, McDonalds spends a great deal of money on television ads. This doesn't mean they ignore their location, facilities, signage, outdoor advertising, and many other marketing tools.

You must also have the time and money to let a marketing plan work. Most plans will not work with a one-time exposure. All good marketing plans require time and repetition.

Marketing is something everyone in your organization must do all the time and every day. Marketing is never done. If you get too busy with the day-to-day operations of your business and quit marketing, you'll wake up one day with no business.

Track the effectiveness of your advertising. You need to know where every customer came from. Write it down so you know, and not just guess. For example, at Duffy's Collectible Cars I knew 22% of our sales came from our web site when I left the company.

When you do find a good plan and theme, stick with it. You'll get sick of it long before the public. Don't be changing for the sake of change or because your sales people want something new.

If you're not comfortable developing and implementing your own marketing plan, buy or hire marketing help. Do not under any circumstances start your business without a marketing plan. Remember the "Build a better mouse trap" myth.

Chapter 8: Market Research

We'll talk about various resources available to someone starting a business in a later chapter, but there are two important elements where resources are scarce. These two areas are market research and marketing in general. It's nice to have help in setting up your books, but it's almost irrelevant if you have no customers, no sales, and no profits.

How do you do the research to determine if there is demand for the product or service you're planning to offer? Hiring a professional market research firm is a good option, if you can afford it, but this kind of professional help is too expensive for most small businesses.

You may have to do the market research yourself. When I say do the research yourself, I mean gather the data. I don't mean going by your perceptions and emotions.

The fact that you would buy or use a particular product or service means nothing, if there aren't enough consumers like you to support your business. On the other hand, the fact that you personally wouldn't use a product or service doesn't mean there isn't a market for that product or service.

Every product, or industry, has a life cycle. When plotted as a graph, this life cycle normally looks like the classic bell curve. Your market research needs to tell you where the product or service you're considering is in its life cycle.

Products or services in the early stages of the life cycle obviously offer the most potential. This doesn't mean that products or services in the declining part of a life cycle are bad.

The harness and saddle industry went into decline after the introduction of the internal combustion engine. This doesn't mean there is no market. Companies making saddles for pleasure riding do very well. The market changed. Be aware of the changes.

◆ ◆ ◆

One of the classic errors I've seen people make is using the local yellow pages for market research. You can look in the yellow pages and see a lot of companies listed offering the same product or service you are considering. Does it mean the market is already saturated, or does it mean that it's a good business? If it means it's a good business, then you just have to decide if your business system will get you your share of the business. You do know that you'll have competition.

If you look in the yellow pages and there's no listing for your product or service, what does it mean? It may simply mean the yellow pages are not a good marketing tool for that product or service. It may mean there's not much competition. It may mean there's not enough demand to support your business.

A good example is Obstetrics & Gynecology physicians. The yellow pages from almost any community will show a disproportionate amount of Obstetrics & Gynecology physicians, but I'm told it usually takes months to get in to see one. The

Obstetrics & Gynecology business must be a good one.

◆ ◆ ◆

Market research should verify demand for your product or service, and identify your potential customer. It must also identify your competition and your competition's strengths and weaknesses. You must have this information to market and compete successfully.

Once you identify your market niche and potential customer, you have to determine how to most effectively market to him or her. There may be a lot of customers who need or want what you have to offer, but if they don't know you exist and what products or services you offer, you can't make a sale.

Telemarketing and canvassing can be a valuable market research tool if you listen carefully to the information gathered. You might even find a new customer or make a sale in some cases. Questionnaires can also help identify your customer and how to market to them.

Market research takes time and money, but it's cheaper than making mistakes as a result of not doing the research beforehand. One example is spending money on advertising that doesn't reach your potential customer. This is a total waste of money.

◆ ◆ ◆

A business associate who we'll call Don once called me about a friend of his who we'll call Jim. Don was concerned because Jim planned to leave a secure and well-paying position in a family owned manufacturing business to start a new business.

Jim planned on starting a lawn care business that

would be primarily mowing. Don imagined this business as a neighborhood boy out mowing lawns with a push mower for spending money.

I told Don there was nothing wrong with the lawn care business if run properly. I told him I had a son who had started a lawn care business doing primarily mowing in both the Midwest and the west coast. My son also sold both these businesses at a profit. I told Don I would talk to Jim.

Jim was in fact starting a lawn care business doing primarily mowing. He'd bought all new equipment with no outside input, except from the sales people selling him the equipment.

He'd run an ad in the major newspaper for the Minneapolis/Saint Paul metro area where he lived to get customers. The Twin Cities market is made up of over 3½ million people in over 180 cities and townships covering a sprawling area of over 6,000 square miles.

Jim told me he liked doing yard work and being outside. This was his total criterion for starting the mowing business. He had no experience in the lawn care business or how the business worked. He also had no idea how to market his business.

Jim had done no market research. He hadn't identified his customers or how to reach them. He also had not identified his competition or how to compete. Jim hadn't even defined the geographic area he'd be servicing except for the Twin Cities metro area.

Without knowing the services his customers needed, Jim had no idea what equipment he needed. I'm sure he'd bought some great shiny new equipment that he would have liked for his own yard.

If Jim had any experience in the lawn care industry, or had done his market research, he'd have known that his customers must be closely concentrated. You make money in that business by performing the service quickly and efficiently. You don't make any money driving from customer to customer. Time on the road eats up time and gas with no profit.

Running an ad in the major metro paper probably wasted his money. This isn't a good way to market a lawn care business. Even if Jim did get customers from the ad, they would be too spread out to be profitable. He would eat up all his profits driving around the Twin Cities. Jim had pretty much guaranteed his failure.

When I talked to Jim, he'd already committed to the business and had no interest in hearing any advice I might have for him. I called Don back and told him he had good cause to be concerned for Jim.

I called Jim several months later, and talked to his wife. She told me Jim was "still doing that business." I could hear the unhappiness and disgust in her voice. I'm sure Jim worked a lot of hours running all over the Twin Cities and not understanding why he wasn't making a profit. Unfortunately, working harder could never make the business profitable with Jim's lack of a good business system.

Jim had no experience in the industry. He didn't have a proven business system. Jim hadn't done his market research. He never identified his customer. He didn't know how to market to his customer. Jim was working *in the business* rather than *running the business*. Jim's business never had a chance to succeed. Its no wonder some people think going into business for yourself is a big risk.

◆ ◆ ◆

It would be nice if market research could guarantee that you would make all the right decisions. Unfortunately, marketing is time sensitive. The market changes every day.

A marketing professor once told me, "By the time you get enough information to be 100% sure you're right, you're wrong because you're too late." This statement is so true that I once had it printed on the back of my business cards when I worked in franchise development.

Market research isn't just important before you start a business. Market research should be part of your ongoing marketing plan, because markets change. Consumers want and need change. Products change. Technology changes. Packaging changes. Distribution channels change. Competitors change. The market continually changes. Everything changes.

I once heard an Earl Nightingale radio program that I still remember. It was called something like "Success is One of The Greatest Causes of Failure." At first, this sounds like a contradiction, but it makes sense.

It's easy for a successful business to get complacent and ignore the changes in the market. By the time sales drop, it's often too late for the business to react. This is sometimes true for entire industries.

Market research should be ongoing. It may be difficult to devote time to research when business is good and you're busy running your business, but ignoring changes in the market could be disastrous.

Since you probably can't afford a professional market research firm, you'll still have to make your own decision based on the information and data you gather. Don't make this decision purely on perception and emotion. Gather all the data and information you can so you can make an "educated guess." You still may have to end up going with your gut.

You can ask friends and relatives, but their perceptions and emotions are probably less fact based than your own. I generally don't recommend asking friends and relatives for their opinion unless it's someone with expertise in a specific area. Then only ask for their opinion in their area of expertise.

Chapter 9: Product Management

An essential part of any marketing plan is defining the product or service you're offering your customers and pricing that product or service. The two most common errors in this area of marketing are trying to be everything to everyone, and trying to compete on price. We'll look at trying to compete on price in a later chapter.

Let's take a look at the mistake of trying to be everything to everybody. This is an easy mistake to make because it is hard to turn away business when you're first starting out.

New companies will often be competing with larger and more established businesses. One effective way to compete is to narrow the product or service you offer. You can now be an expert with what you offer. People like to deal with experts. Don't try to be everything to everyone.

◆　◆　◆

I managed a collector car business located on a dead end street called Classic Car Court. A restaurant called the Rag Top Diner stood on the corner. The location wasn't great, but had good traffic and visibility from the interstate highway. The collector car showroom also provided additional traffic.

The name "Rag Top" is slang for a convertible and fit the collector car image. The Diner was decorated in a 1950's motif with a lot of chrome and memorabilia.

The diner specialized in hamburgers and fries. They had a soda fountain and served great shakes. They also opened for breakfast, serving traditional breakfasts. The menu was pretty basic, but they did what they did very well. For example, they never used frozen fries or hamburgers.

The diner stayed packed from six in the morning until dark. They cut a door in the wall to the connecting building and added an additional dining room. A second Rag Top Diner opened in a better location across town. It also stayed packed from early morning until dark.

The owners of the diners were delighted. They had big ideas. They even planned on franchising. I tried to tell them in a nice way that they'd better get some professional advice from someone that knew something about franchising and franchise development.

Both diners were doing great, but they had little business after dark. In the summer, this meant they were busy until 9:00 in the evening, but during the winter months they had hardly any business after 6:00 in the evening.

The management decided to change their menu and operation in order to attract the evening dinner business. They made the changes. They lost their niche market, and were forced to compete with every other restaurant, café, and diner in town.

The Rag Top Diners were never successful in attracting the dinner business. They also lost their daytime business. In a few years, both diners were closed. The one with the best location now houses a successful food franchise. The one in the poorer location now houses a small church.

The Rag Top Diner should never have been concerned with the dinner business. They shouldn't have tried to be all things to all people. If they would have stayed with the 50's image serving hamburgers, fries, and malts they might still be in business and making money today.

◆ ◆ ◆

I once worked as a plant manager for a recreational vehicle plant that produced a full line of pickup toppers and covers. The least expensive and highest volume was the all-aluminum cover. The wood slant-side cover looked the same as an aluminum cover, but had a wood frame and plywood interior, and was higher priced.

We also produced a cover called a Deluxe Wood Topper, which was more of a camper. It had a heavy 2" wood frame with straight sides. It had a plywood interior and came fully insulated. We offered it in various heights that sometimes extended forward over the top of the pickup cab.

The last cover, a fiberglass reinforced plastic laminate cover, was more streamlined and had windows with rounded instead of square corners. It came only in white unless painted, and was the most expensive.

When I took over as plant manager, we were selling about 40 units a day. The problem was, we were only producing 20 units a day. Our backlog of orders continued getting bigger. Our delivery schedules got pushed further and further out. Our dealers were screaming for product. We were losing sales because we couldn't supply the product in a timely manner. Growth is not always good. It can create problems.

I had to make several changes over the next three months to double production. One major change was to clean up the product line. Up to that time we had tried to give our dealers anything and everything they wanted. We literally had dozens of options for every cover and topper we manufactured. This made purchasing, costing, pricing, inventory control, and production a nightmare.

I evaluated our sales for the last year. Any options ordered over 50% of the time were made standard equipment. Any option ordered less than 20% of the time was dropped. The prices of the remaining options increased about 50%.

We lost a few sales because of limiting the options, but not many. Some dealers complained, but soon loved the new product line, because the change made it easier for the dealers to order and stock a full inventory. It made it less confusing for their customers, and as a result easier to close the sale.

The number of components used in production were reduced radically. For example, the front window of the topper that butts up to the pickup cab. When I took over as plant manager, we were using over two-dozen slightly different front windows, and each had a different cost.

I eliminated all but four. We had a square fixed and a square slider window. We had a fixed and slider window with rounded corners for the fiberglass reinforced acrylic cover.

This change made a huge difference in purchasing and inventory control. It made production less complicated. It made costing and pricing much easier. I actually lowered costs because we could now buy each of the remaining front windows in higher quantities.

You cannot be everything to everyone. You must define your product or service. This is the best way to serve your customer and make a profit.

◆　◆　◆

I later worked as a consultant to revise the product line, costing, purchasing, and inventory control for a couple other recreational vehicle manufacturers. One of the companies that hired me had previously hired another consulting firm. They'd paid this firm a lot of money.

When I first met with the company, they gave me a typed report about four inches thick from the previous firm. After scanning the report, it became quite clear that there was a lot of rhetoric, but no real solutions.

My recommendation was simple. Improve profits by redefining the product line, and thus reducing inventory and inventory control problems. This in turn would simplify purchasing, costing, and manufacturing. My total recommendation only took one typed page. Implementation took a little longer.

Once the manufacturer and their dealers understood that they could not supply everyone's needs, they loved the new product line. I understand that it is very hard to pass on potential business even though that business is not profitable.

◆   ◆   ◆

At the Ford-Mercury dealership, I had a neighbor and friend who owned and operated some pharmacies and drug stores. Gary was educated as a pharmacist and had no formal business training, but he was very bright and a good businessman.

Gary had some simple philosophies about business. If he stocked a product in his stores, he had the best selection of that product in town, or he didn't stock the product at all. Gary also felt that any advertising without price was a waste of money.

Gary was a very successful businessman with his drug stores. He became a pioneer in the business of renting medical equipment for home use.

Remember, identify your niche market, specialize, and do what your do well. Be an expert with what you do. You can't be everything to everyone. This philosophy is one of the reasons franchises are successful.

◆   ◆   ◆

Product management can also be as simple as displaying your product in such a way that the customer who sees it wants to purchase it. We must remember that a large percentage of sales are impulse buys for customers.

Even an old fart like me can barely remember the days when the customer went into a general store, grocery store, or hardware store and told the proprietor what they wanted. The proprietor then went to get the item or items to complete the sale.

Those days are gone except for the movies.

Today's consumer wants to see, feel, and touch the merchandise. This requires larger and brighter facilities. This type of merchandising also saves on labor.

Chapter 10: Price

Offer your customer value, not price. Price is very important, but if you think you're going to compete on price alone, forget it. You still have to market your product or service and make money. Your competitors are probably in a much better position for a price war than you are. They have an established customer base. They have the advantage of an established volume. They may have cash reserves for the price war with you.

◆　◆　◆

In college, I once read a case study that I found very interesting. I don't remember the details, but I'll generalize.

A major small appliance manufacturer had developed a product that we'll call an electric toothbrush. With the manufacturing cost at that time, they could profitably sell the electric toothbrush for $19.95. They introduced the product and sales were very disappointing.

After doing some market research, they discovered that the public didn't feel that the electric toothbrush could be a quality product if it only cost $19.95. The public related quality to the price.

The manufacturer recalled all the electric toothbrushes and put them in a warehouse. After two years they reintroduced the same product into the marketplace with a $39.95 price. The product sold like hot cakes. The public bought the product at the higher price because they then had a perception of quality.

◆　◆　◆

As I mentioned, I now live on a lake in Wisconsin. The area is somewhat of a resort area. More than half the houses are summer homes with seasonal residents.

I know of an individual who started a landscaping business in the area. He tracked down the mailing address for the owners of all the homes on the lakes in the area. He then mailed them a flyer promoting his service. The flyer stated he would beat anyone's price for lawn care.

The lack of responses confused him. When we think about it, why would anyone respond to his flyer? He said he was cheap. He didn't say he provided a quality service.

Why would anyone who can afford a summer home on a lake be interested in cheap lawn care? If his flyer had said he offered the highest quality lawn care in the area instead of saying he would beat any price, he probably would have gotten calls and some new customers.

A higher price means better quality to many people. I can just hear how skeptical some of you are of this statement. Some of you think you only pay for quality. Don't kid yourself. We all pay a premium for name, image, and packaging every day. Sometimes our only gauge of the quality is the price.

I think a product like perfume is one of the best examples. If perfume were priced based on production cost and a fair markup, most brands would sell for a couple dollars. Packaging, advertising, the retail outlet, and the price determine the perceived value.

If I buy a new shirt for $45 at one store and the identical shirt for $25 at another store, is the one for $45 better? Some people will swear it is better.

It may actually have greater value in spite of being identical products. The store, location, selection, presentation, and sales personnel all contribute to the value, and may indeed command a higher price. Isn't marketing and image great?

◆　◆　◆

When in the Ford-Mercury dealership, I found it interesting that a replacement part for a Ford, Mercury, and Lincoln had three different part numbers and three different prices in spite of it being the same exact part in some cases. The Lincoln owner expected to pay more for a part for their Lincoln than the same part for a Mercury or a Ford. The Mercury owner expected to pay more for their part than the same part for a Ford. Ford Motor Company was kind enough to oblige them.

Every year at the dealership, I tried to give cars away at true invoice cost for one day. This wasn't a bait and switch or a gimmick in any way. We'll talk about bait and switch in the chapter on advertising.

I sold cars at my true cost for one day. I ran the sale from 9:00 a.m. to 9:00 p.m. I promoted the sale with full-page ads in both papers in the area. I would put the true invoice cost on the windshield of every car with white shoe polish.

The interesting part is that I sold very few cars at the sale price on the sale day. I did sell cars as a result of the sale, but not on that day at that price.

I remember a woman looking at a car and talking

to the salesman as I wiped the price off the windshield at 9:00 one night. She said she had to think about it. I told her the price would be $300 higher in the morning. She said she understood. Two days later she came back and paid the additional $300 without even arguing.

Why did I run a one-day sale every year that cost me money? I ran the sale for two reasons. One: it promoted the dealership. Two: it reminded my sales staff and I that price wasn't really that big a part of the buying decision. The consumer was just not that price conscious. They just wanted to feel they'd gotten a good buy.

I also learned another important lesson of value versus price in the car dealership. We offered tune-ups for our customers in our service department. I kept getting complaints that our prices were too high. The menu-pricing concept didn't existed for automobile service at that time.

I looked over several service invoices and saw all the parts listed individually with the appropriate prices. I found the problem with the labor charge. The invoice just said "Tune Up" with the appropriate dollar amount. We changed the invoice to list about two-dozen services performed with a tune-up instead of just saying "Tune Up." The price remained the same. Our customer now felt they were getting great value for their money.

We hadn't changed the service. We'd just shown the customer what services we'd performed for him or her. Don't make the mistake of assuming the customer knows the value of your product or service. They probably don't. If they understood everything you are doing for them, they might not even need your product or service. They could do it themselves.

❖   ❖   ❖

I previously mentioned being a plant manager for a manufacturing plant producing pickup covers. I first went to work for the company as sales manager. The chairman of the board wanted to buy the market with price competition.

I normally don't like price competition. I feel it's risky and often very expensive. I told the chairman of the board I would agree to the price competition if he would commit the financial resources and reserves I felt might be needed for the complete marketing plan. I stressed that the reserves had to be available at my discretion with "no questions asked." He agreed.

We were able to buy and dominate the eight states we considered our market. Once we controlled the market and proved ourselves to our dealers, we started to raise our prices.

Price collusion is illegal, but every time I raised our prices, I simply sent a new price list to all of our competitors. I wanted them to know our prices. Mailing them a new price list saved them the time and hassle of learning our new prices in the marketplace.

One competitor decided to not follow our lead and compete in price. He was a small regional producer. I dropped my prices to below cost for dealers in his area. I could afford to do this in a small percentage of my market and absorb the loss, but it was his entire market and he couldn't afford to compete. He quickly learned that he didn't want a price war with a larger and better-financed competitor.

We offered special pricing to some of our largest dealers. It was normal in the industry to give some of the largest volume dealers special pricing or discounts. When we bought the market, we had ten large dealers that were strictly overhead accounts. Basically, this meant we weren't making any money off them.

I became the plant manager after we increased our dealer organization and sales. We increased our plant capacity to meet sales.

I soon decided to increase the price to the ten overhead accounts. I called in my sales manager and told him my intentions. I told him that with the price increase I proposed, I expected to lose all ten dealers. This decision didn't make my sales manager happy, but he understood why I chose to do it.

The interesting thing is that we'd proven ourselves to the ten dealers by this time. We only lost two of the ten dealers. Eight dealers stayed with us at the new price. My sales manager and I were much happier with eight large dealers that made us money than ten large dealers that didn't make us any money.

◆   ◆   ◆

Shipping costs can be an important part of the pricing strategy. If your customers are located over a wide geographic area, it may be a critical part of your pricing strategy. This can be very important with today's Internet business.

Recently at an entrepreneur's club meeting, one of the guest speakers was a woman who, with husband, raised, processed, and sold grass fed buffalo meat. This is a very unique niche market. Buffalo meat is unique, and some buffalo is fed-out on corn or grain.

Grass fed buffalo meat is very unique and low fat.

They were located in the Midwest, but most of their customers came from their web site and were located on both the east and west coasts. The problem they faced was the cost of shipping. The shipping cost often ran as high as 75% of the cost of the meat. The web site gave the meat cost, but the customer had to call for the cost to ship the product. The fact the customer had to call for shipping costs made it harder to make the purchase and probably cost sales.

When the customers did call, two out of three cancelled the order when told the shipping cost. The owners finally realized that the customers perceived no value in the cost of the shipping.

They resolved the problem by doubling the price of the meat to build in the shipping cost. They now quoted a flat shipping and packaging charge of $15.95 on all orders over $50. The customer could now place an order on line without having to call for the shipping charge. Most customers expected to pay some shipping and packaging charge for a product as perishable as meat, and considered $15.95 reasonable.

There now was a perception of value added to the product. The customer now would be eating a $40 buffalo steak instead of a $20 buffalo steak with a $15 delivery charge. Still the same grass fed buffalo steak. The price had increased $5, but the perception of value had increased. Sales tripled.

Think about the $5 increase in price for a minute. In most cases, this became pure profit. Tripling sales and increasing profit margin at the same time did not make the owners unhappy.

Never forget that perception of value has little or nothing to do with your profit margin. Remember how the customer didn't know the difference when I offered to sell cars at my true cost.

◆ ◆ ◆

I have to mention estimates as an important part of pricing in many businesses. If your business gives estimates, always give a firm estimate. The estimate should be in writing with an expiration date.

Never give a ballpark estimate. This is a *lose-lose* situation. The customer often says, "Just give me some idea. I won't hold you to it." Don't do it. Don't ever do it. Do not fall into this trap.

If you give a high estimate, the customer will never contact you again, and why should they. You were too high. If you are low, they may come back, but when you give them a firm estimate, they will say, "but you said." Never believe the customer "won't hold you to it" if you give them a low ballpark estimate.

In the car business, my customers often wanted some idea of the value of their trade. If I gave them a ballpark, I lost. If I gave a low estimate of their trade, I would never see them again. If I gave them a high figure for their trade, I had a problem later as they would hold me to what I had said. There is no winning with ballpark estimates.

The car business is unique in that many dealers will intentionally give a low-ball trade difference, or intentionally over-state the value of the trade-in if they think the customer is shopping. The dealer will do this intentionally with the idea that the customer cannot match the deal, and will have to come back to the dealership. It's then up to the salesman to make up some excuse about the *mistake* and close the customer.

Many businesses do use some variation on the low-ball successfully. I've never employed this practice, and I don't recommend it. I feel it hurts your reputation in the long run.

◆　◆　◆

I had a friend who was a Firestone tire dealer. I'll talk more about his operation later in this book. John used to say he lost money on every tire he sold, but he made it up on volume. Somehow, I don't think it works that way.

In Dan Kennedy's book *No B.S. Wealth Attraction for Entrepreneurs,* he states that when he does individual consulting, his recommendations normally include increasing the price. He sometimes recommends large price increases.

Sometimes the easiest way to increase profits is to increase margins. It's feasible that the price increase may even increase sales, as the public may perceive higher quality.

I recently watched an episode of "Shark Tank" on TV. If you are not familiar with the show, it's about a group of wealthy individuals (sharks) that may or may not offer to finance entrepreneurs' business ideas.

I may have the details wrong, but on one episode an entrepreneur had a high end product he sold for around $300. All the sharks were in agreement the price for the product should be $1,200. This price better fit the quality image of the product.

If the gross profit was $100 with a selling price of $300, the gross profit margin is now $1,000 with a selling price of $1,200. With this kind of margin, it takes a lot less sales to be profitable.

Chapter 11: Name, Logo & Image

Your name and logo are definitely an important part of any marketing plan. Give some thought to your business name. Your name and logo should be easily identified and be descriptive of your business. *Cute* or *Catchy* is nice, but not if it doesn't describe your business.

I must be old fashion, but I have a real problem with some of the names in the marketplace today. It's very popular today with companies to have logos that are not descriptive of who the company is or what they do. I think this is a big mistake.

No acronyms please. What is ING for a company name? It took a fortune in TV advertising just to make the public aware they offered financial services.

McDonalds' *Golden Arches* work very well, but it took a lot of years, a lot of marketing, and a fortune in advertising to make it the recognizable image it is today. Most of you can't afford this unless you're part of a franchise organization.

A name should present an image. It should be easy to pronounce. It should also look good in print. These three things are the minimum requirements for a name.

◆   ◆   ◆

As I mentioned, I was a Ford-Mercury dealer in a previous life. I actually bought the dealership and had the franchise awarded while still in graduate school for my MBA.

At the time, I was doing some individual study with the professor of advertising. He got very interested with my purchase of the Ford-Mercury dealership. We made picking a name for the dealership a project for two of his classes.

We considered dozens of names. The name had to meet many criteria. The name had to be simple, personal, identify the business, be easy to pronounce, and look good in print. The result was Lee Motors, Inc. Most people wouldn't think any thought had gone into selecting the name, when in fact, the name resulted from extensive research and study.

We then designed a logo to go under the name. Simply stated, "Your (Ford Mercury Sign) Dealer." This logo further described the business and the image we wanted.

◆　◆　◆

I think a logo should say something or present some image. I do not understand graphics that say nothing. At least the golden arches say something. I think having a logo that is some form of modern art is a total waste.

Ask yourself a couple questions about your logo. First of all, do you need one? If you do want or need a logo, what should it say, and what image should it project?

When I started Collectible Car Showcase, I picked the name and designed the logo. I picked the name because we were in the collectible car business and we had an indoor showroom that displayed more than 100 cars. I thought the name fit the business.

The circular logo, a steering wheel, had the name

and location incorporated in the steering wheel. We chose turquoise and pink as the colors, which were popular and unique to cars of the 1950's.

I think the logo presented an image for the business. It also didn't need a lot of explanation.

◆　◆　◆

There are always exceptions. We had a restaurant in our area named "The Pickled Trout." This name clearly does not say the business is a restaurant, but it does present a distinct image.

We have another restaurant in our area that's been in this resort area since the 1920s. It's located on Lake Pokegama with access by both land and water. It's been called Pokegama Inn and has had a good reputation for over eighty years. New owners bought the Pokegama Inn and changed the name. Not a smart move. Local people will probably call it Pokegama Inn for years anyway. Change is tough for some of us old farts.

◆　◆　◆

I recommend picking a name and logo that describes your business and presents an image you want for your business. Leave the modern art and acronyms that have no meaning or need explanation to someone who can afford a huge advertising budget.

Chapter 12: Location & Signage

Finding the right location for your business is critical to your success. The first question is, will your customer come to your place of business, or will you go to your customer?

Some businesses need a retail facility that has high traffic count. This could be foot traffic in a retail mall, or vehicle traffic. The vehicle traffic can be past a strip mall or a stand-alone facility.

The old real estate saying that the three most important things are location, location, and location, now becomes relevant. You will pay a premium for a facility in a location that has high traffic, high visibility, and easy access. This type of real estate is expensive, but it might be critical to the success of your business.

◆ ◆ ◆

If your customer comes to you, you will need more of a premium location than if you go to your customer. If your customer comes to you, do you need high visibility, high car count, high foot traffic, easy access, convenient parking, and/or drive-up capability? There may be a dozen other questions you need to ask. You may need high visibility, but not easy access. You may need easy access, but not high visibility. Don't commit to paying for both if you don't need both.

Space in an enclosed mall will cost more than in a strip mall, and both will cost more than space in a warehouse area or space in an industrial area. Saving money on a poor location will only cost you money in the long run if your customers can't find you. You need to be sure to meet your needs, but not pay for a location you don't need. This is a very important, long-term fixed overhead commitment we're talking about.

If your customer seldom or never comes to your business, you can rent warehouse space that's hard to find in a cheap part of town. You also may need more storage space and the cost per square foot of warehouse space will be cheaper than retail space.

Your customer may never visit your place of business, but your needs will still vary depending on employee access, parking, and other considerations. It should be a safe area of town. It also should be conveniently located to where you are conducting business.

I have a relative that has a successful used car business. It's unique by old standards, as he's located in a hard to find location in an industrial park. He doesn't have the traditional business from drive-by traffic.

His business comes almost totally from Internet advertising. This is also his major expense. The customer comes to the place of business by appointment in most cases, and is given detailed instructions for finding the business.

There is no need for a high priced location. The facility does need a clean, professional image to gain the customer's confidence.

He recently moved to a different facility in the same area. The reason for the move was to gain a location with a security fence. He'd learned that being located in an area with little traffic at night presented a theft problem. Vehicles were not stolen, but their various parts were. Pickup tailgates were a favorite and expensive item stolen. Security can be a consideration.

◆ ◆ ◆

I knew a collectible car dealer in a crowded and hard to find part of Chicago. Don had a problem with space for both customer parking and vehicle inventory display. He also had a large advertising budget.

Eventually, Don bought a high priced piece of real estate with a lot of space and high visibility from Interstate 94 north of Chicago over the Wisconsin line. Don said the real estate was expensive, but with the exposure from I-94, he no longer had to spend much on advertising. He also no longer had a space problem for inventory and parking.

◆ ◆ ◆

Individual businesses present special location considerations that we might never think of without help or prior experience in that specific business. I once did some consulting work for a dry cleaning franchise. They knew that a location needed to be on a road with high traffic. It also needed easy access and convenient parking and maybe even a drive-up option.

This all makes sense. However, what never occurred to me was that it needed to be on the *to work* side of the road. People will not cross the road to drop off their laundry on their way to work. They have to cross the road on their way home to pick up the clothes anyway, but they normally are not so rushed on the way home. I never would have thought of this. Would you?

Many commercial leases are done on what is called *Triple Net*. What this means is that in addition to your lease payment, you also pay all utilities, taxes, and maintenance.

You'll also probably be responsible for any *build-out* costs. This means you'll be renting an empty shell and all costs to finish the space are yours. This can be a considerable investment, as you must project an attractive image to your customer.

When you're shopping for a location or facility, always keep more than one option available. You will have a first choice, as you should, but keep working on your second choice too. It may be smart in some cases to also keep working on your third choice. If you concentrate only on your first choice, you have no leverage to use in your lease negotiations. If you don't get your first choice for some reason, and you haven't continued to work on your second and third, you will essentially be starting over and have lost months. Time is money.

I had one client who went in to sign his lease one morning. He had an appointment to sign the contract for the build-out with the contractor that afternoon. Everything was ready to go.

When he got to the developer's office, the developer told him he'd decided to lease the property to someone else. The developer had been stringing him along all the time and knew he hoped to rent the property to someone else.

Unfortunately, my client had not taken my advice. He'd believed and trusted the developer, and had not pursued any other locations. People in business sometimes are not totally truthful. Protect yourself.

◆ ◆ ◆

The signs for your retail facility may be a very important part of your marketing plan. It may be the only way your customer finds your business. What do you want your sign to do?

A new restaurant opened on one of the six connected lakes where we live. The new owner wanted an illuminated sign on the front of the restaurant large enough to be easily visible from the other side of the lake and the bridge where the lake connects to another lake.

The sign needed to be visible to both boat traffic coming under the bridge, and vehicle traffic crossing over the bridge. With this objective in mind, the size of the sign could be computed mathematically.

Signage costs are also your responsibility in most cases. Signs are surprisingly expensive. Know the sign cost before signing the lease. You must also check that zoning will allow the signage you want to install. Don't make the mistake of thinking the sign zoning will make any sense. We all should know that this is not the way government works.

I believe there was a time when one northern Chicago suburb didn't allow any signs except black and white. They also had severe restrictions on size. The *Golden Arches* were not golden in this town. I don't know if that's still the case today. Government does some weird things.

You'll have to work with the city zoning commission to get the facility and signs you need and want. This means you may have to play their game.

Remember to work with the planning commission, and to not be confrontational. There's nothing wrong with asking for more than you think you'll get. You may reach a happy compromise. We'll talk more about working with local bureaucrats in the Insurance & Government Regulations chapter.

◆　◆　◆

Your business signs may, and in many cases should, extend beyond your physical facility. If your business is a mobile business that goes to the customer, that vehicle may be your sign. It can be a rolling billboard.

Vehicle graphics now can be as simple as lettering, or as extensive as full color wraps with today's technology. Most of us have seen large city buses completely covered with full color wraps.

When I had the Ford-Mercury dealership, there was a very successful real estate company in a neighboring town. We'll call the Realtor that owned the company Fred. Fred controlled over 50% of the real estate market in this town.

Fred did a very good job marketing his company. Fred always spent 20% of company commissions on advertising.

Fred offered to pay his sales associates a monthly car allowance if their vehicle met certain company guidelines. The vehicle had to be a solid red station wagon not over a few years old. The station wagon had to have full wheel covers, white wall tires, and a roof luggage rack. Fred then provided white company graphics for the sides of the vehicle.

Only about a third of Fred's sales associates took

advantage of this program, but it was enough to make an impact in the market place. When you asked the public how many of these red wagons were running around, the response would be something like ten times the actual number.

This phenomenon is called synergism. We perceive something larger than the actual sum of the individual parts; in this case, the public thought there were many more station wagons than there actually were.

◆   ◆   ◆

It doesn't make sense to spend a lot of money on signs for your building if your customers never come to your building. You may even run your business out of your home. You certainly won't want a sign on your home.

If you run your business out of your home, some residential neighborhoods have regulations restricting parking of business vehicles. Be sure you can park your rolling billboard at your home. If not, you will have to rent parking or garage space at another convenient location.

Chapter 13: Facilities & Image

You may question how your facilities are part of your marketing plan. Your facility is definitely included under my definition of marketing as it establishes your business image and how your customer perceives you and your business.

Some businesses can be run out of a home office, and/or garage. If your business falls into this category, it will lower start-up costs and reduce lead-time. Don't make the mistake of trying to run the business out of an area of the house used by other family members.

You may be able to run your business out of your home, but you'll need some storage area. The storage area may be in your house or garage, but again, make sure it's secure and not used by other family members.

You may need to rent a storage unit. Make sure it's conveniently located near your home if you need to go there often. Time spent on the road probably doesn't make you any money.

Your business may utilize a mobile unit. If this is the case, you still may need storage. You'll also need parking and/or garage space for your vehicle.

If your business uses vehicles, identification and signage is very important, as we've already discussed. Your company vehicles can be rolling billboards.

◆ ◆ ◆

You may want to keep your business separate from your home for a variety of reasons. You may just need a small office space. This space can be in a large office building.

One popular option for small businesses today is the shared office concept. You rent an office or cubicle for your personal use. This is usually fully furnished and equipped.

You then share a receptionist and reception area. You may have meeting rooms and conference rooms available as needed. Normally, secretarial services, copy machines, and mail services are available on an as-needed basis.

This option can give you a prestigious location and image at a fraction of the cost. I've known people to use the address, phone service, and meeting rooms when they never even had a cubicle in the building.

The image of your physical facility may be critical to your success. If your customer comes to your place of business, it must be clean, neat, efficient, well lit, and attractive. Today's consumer will not do business where the facility doesn't appear efficient and aesthetically pleasing. When we work in the same place every day, it's easy to overlook poor housekeeping. Don't be fooled into thinking your customer will overlook the same.

If your customer doesn't come to your place of business it only has to be clean, neat, efficient, well lit, and attractive. Please note all the differences. Oops, I don't see any. Poor housekeeping does not promote efficiency.

◆ ◆ ◆

McDonalds is a very successful franchise. Their *Golden Arches* are well known around the world. Part of their success is that McDonalds restaurants are clean. It's a strong requirement of the franchise. There's a story that when Ray Kroc, the founder of McDonalds, would attend a grand opening, he would often be found in the parking lot picking up trash. Ray Kroc knew the value of having a clean and neat place of business.

When I opened the Sparks Computerized Car Care in the Chicago area, I made a point of being picky about maintaining a neat and clean place of business. This isn't always easy in the automotive repair business as the very nature of automobile service is frequently working with dirt, oil, and grease.

Once when mopping the floor in the shop, a salesman walked up to me and said he assumed I was the owner since I was mopping the floor in the shop. I soon taught all my employees the value of a clean place of business.

We were doing a diagnostic test on a woman's car once when she asked me where we did the actual work on the cars. She assumed that since the shop looked so neat and clean, we did the work somewhere else. When I informed her that this is where we preformed the work, we had a new customer for all her automotive service needs. She appreciated getting a clean car back after service with no grease on the floor mats or steering wheel.

The facility must be neat and efficient. I mean the entire facility. Not just what the customer sees. Plan the traffic flow for both customers and staff.

Plan for storage. Storage is the most often overlooked facility need. Everything should have a place and everything should be in its place. If things are just lying around, it looks messy and people will waste time looking for things.

Time wasted looking for anything is one of my pet peeves. There's probably nothing less productive. If time is money, time wasted looking for something is one of the biggest wastes of time and money I can think of.

When I say neat, this includes desks. Yes, I have heard the, "It looks messy, but I know where everything is" comment. I've also observed these same people wasting a lot of time looking for things. Some things are found eventually, and some are never found when needed. If you are one of these "It only looks messy" people, face reality and quit kidding yourself.

◆ ◆ ◆

The last thing I want to say about finding and getting your facility ready to open is that it will cost more and take longer than you think.

I had a couple for clients that we'll call Rick and Ann. They decided what business they wanted in May. Rick would stay in his job and Ann would quit hers to run the business.

They planned on opening by the first of October. They considered four months more than enough time to find a location, negotiate the lease, and do the build-out. Ann planned to give notice to her employer that she would be quitting in September. I told her not to tell her employer until they got closer to opening as it might take longer than they expected.

They had their grand opening in June the following year and there were no major problems.

They just had a lot of normal minor problems. Since Ann didn't quit her job prematurely, she continued to have that income for an additional six months.

Always assume it will take longer and cost more than you think it should. It will. Count on it.

Chapter 14: Sales

I have heard some people say sales and marketing are two separate things. With my definition of marketing, sales is a part of marketing. It may be an essential part of marketing in some business systems, but it is still only one part of the total marketing plan.

There's a saying that "Advertising creates sales," but some people say, "Sales create advertising." There is truth in both statements.

There's another old saying that, "Nothing happens in business until somebody makes a sale." Both sales and advertising are part of the marketing plan.

We need to spend time on sales and sales techniques for two reasons. First, sales are an important part of your business. You need to evaluate the type of sales needed in your business. You also need to evaluate the role you'll play in the sales for your business.

The second reason you need to be aware of different sales techniques is that as you are investigating your various business possibilities, people will be trying to sell you something. People will try to sell you on those businesses that make them money. These businesses may not be the best fit for you. You need to be aware of the sales techniques being used. There is a saying that "A good salesman is a sucker for a good sales pitch." Every business has sales or marketing of some sort. How much and what type will be an important part of your decision in selecting a business.

You need to be perfectly honest about your sales ability. Do you have a sales personality or not? Don't put yourself in a sales role if you won't be happy in it.

One of the hardest aspects of sales is the rejection when the prospect does not buy. I've heard people say they can sell if it's something they believe in strongly. The problem with this is that if you believe in the product or service strongly, it makes the rejection even worse when you don't complete the sale.

◆　◆　◆

As a general rule, the rejection is worse and more frequent when you're in a cold call situation than when the potential customer is coming to you. Cold calling with telephone marketing will result in the highest rejection rate. A retail sales clerk will seldom experience the same level of rejection.

Most people think cold calling, either on the phone or in person, is one of the hardest types of sales. Telemarketing is the current term for cold calling on the phone. Face-to face cold calls may be called *door knocking* or canvassing.

Most people teaching cold call sales techniques will tell you to talk to the owner, chief executive officer, chief operating officer, or the person in charge. I don't feel this is always good advice.

I'll later discuss a job one of my sons had selling training programs by phone. When he told me how he'd been trained to only talk to the person in charge, I responded, "Bull!" I told him to talk to whoever could tell him who the real decision makers in the company were for the service he offered.

♦ ♦ ♦

There are many sales approaches. They normally fall into one of six categories. They are:

1. Solving a prospect's problem.

2. Selling features and benefits.

3. The negative sales approach.

4. The limited opportunity approach.

5. The hype sales approach.

6. The assumptive sales approach.

Often, a good sales presentation will utilize more than one of these approaches.

♦ ♦ ♦

I think solving a prospect's problem is the easiest and most rewarding. It does require listening to learn and understand your customer's problem. It also requires you to have the knowledge and resources to solve the customer's problem.

The solution may be so unique your customer has never thought of it before. If the solution you're proposing is new, you must get your customer's trust and confidence.

I had a customer who was a rural mail carrier when I was a car dealer. He also delivered newspapers to several surrounding towns. He made good money, but he *used up* his car. He'd put on a lot of miles and many of them on gravel roads and often in bad conditions. It cost him a fortune to trade every year.

He thought he needed a new car every year for reliability. He traded in a one year-old, high mileage used car that had seen a lot of hard use on gravel roads in all kinds of weather. I hated to see Jack come in every year, because I had to wholesale his high mileage, one-year-old trade. Jack was never happy with what it cost him every year, and I wasn't happy because I didn't make any money either.

After the first year, I suggested an alternative. I worked him into a new trade cycle. I sold lease cars to a local airport rental every year. I took several nice low mileage rentals back in on trade every year.

I suggested he buy one of these every year and give it to his wife to drive, as she didn't put on many miles. The second year, he would give his wife another year old rental car and take her old one for work. The third year, he would trade the three year-old car on a one year-old rental car.

With this trade cycle Jack's wife got a nicely equipped, low mileage, one-year-old car every year. Jack got a nicely equipped low mileage, two year-old car every year for work. Jack then traded in a saleable three year-old car with average miles.

This made Jack happy because we cut his annual car replacement cost in half, and he still had reliable, comfortable transportation. It made me happy because I now had a happy customer, and I could make a reasonable profit.

◆ ◆ ◆

Selling features and benefits is probably the most common sales approach. We've already addressed this in general marketing. Some people will also say this is the most respectable sales approach, as you're not trying to sell somebody something they don't need. This doesn't mean ignoring the emotional appeal.

You must show the customer how they will benefit from the product. The product or service may save the customer time or money. It may improve the customer's quality of life. You may be selling to other businesses and your product or service will improve the quality of the product or service that business offers their customers.

One variation on selling benefits is to suggest that not buying the product or service will in some way be detrimental to the prospect's family or business. An example would be the encyclopedia sales person. The sales person would explain how the product would benefit the prospect's children in school. The negative twist would be suggesting that the children would not be able to compete in school or have the opportunity to go to college without the encyclopedias.

◆　◆　◆

The next sales approach is the *Negative* sale. This is often called a *take-away*. The product or service is offered and then taken away. The idea is that the opportunity, product, or service is only offered to prospects that qualify in some way.

The objective is to make the prospect feel they are one of the lucky ones who qualify for this opportunity. The reality is that the only qualification in most cases is that the prospect has the money to buy what is being sold.

Another aspect of the negative sale is not engaging

your competition. As sales manager for the recreational vehicle manufacturer, part of my job was to find new dealers. No one with our company had been able to sell the largest pickup cover dealer in the state. We'll call this dealer Dean.

I stopped into Dean's RV business one night in jeans as a customer to look over the operation. The next morning, I made a call dressed in casual business attire that fit this dealer. In this business, I might change clothes three times in one day to fit the dealer. Sometimes I'd wear a leisure suit. How bad does that date me?

Dean had one pickup cover salesman in his office. Another pickup cover salesman stood waiting in the reception area. A third pickup cover salesman had a 40' trailer loaded with pickup covers he was trying to sell.

When Dean came out to greet me, I offered him my card, and said, "It looks like you have pickup cover salesmen coming out of your ears. I'll stop back later." I went for a leisurely breakfast and returned.

When I returned, all the salesmen had left. Dean came out of the office to greet me. He said, "I suppose you have a better product for less money." I responded, "No, we make a piece of shit like most people, and we're probably higher priced."

Dean looked shocked. When the shock effect had worn off, I continued. "This is what I can do for you." I talked about ways I could help his business, but I never mentioned a better product or price.

Dean ordered two semi-trailer loads. I then told him how I'd work with him in the future. I explained that I didn't have time to be stopping in and wasting his time. I explained that I'd be in my office every Monday if he wanted to call. I told him who to talk to in our office if I was not there. He could also leave a message at the office and I'd get back to him within twenty-four hours. This was before cell phones. I told you I was an old fart.

I never promised him anything we couldn't deliver. In six months, we were supplying eighty percent of his product.

◆　◆　◆

The *Limited Opportunity* sales approach is just that. When the product, service, or opportunity you're offering is sold, it's gone. There won't be an opportunity to buy at a later date.

There are many examples of this, like discontinued production. You won't be able to buy new Oldsmobiles, Pontiacs, Plymouths, or Ford Ranger pickups after current inventories are sold. None of these are made any more.

This is also true when you're giving an exclusive for a specific area. Franchisors often define an exclusive area when a franchise is awarded. Once that area is awarded, it's gone.

Don't try to create or tell your prospect it's a limited opportunity when it's not true. This lie, as most lies, will hurt you in the long run.

◆　◆　◆

I call the next approach the *Rah-Rah* approach. The *Rah-Rah* or hype sale is simply to create excitement. Make the prospect think this opportunity is the greatest thing since sliced bread. This approach appeals to the emotions and deals very little with facts.

It works amazingly well with people in the right circumstance.

People like to feel they're part of something big and exciting. They like to be associated with other successful people. Large meetings and conventions with lots of people, noise, glitter, and excitement are great motivators for people.

There's nothing wrong with this approach, but as a prospect, don't get caught up in the excitement and buy without properly validating the opportunity. What else is involved in the business other than this exciting get together?

I'm not personally a fan of what I call the *Rah-Rah* sales approach and I've been involved in some very good ones. We once taped $100 bills under some of the front seats in an auditorium to get people sitting up front and involved. This was in the 1970s when a $100 dollar bill was impressive. I don't mean to imply that I don't advocate or believe in appealing to a customer's emotional buying decisions.

Multi-level marketing uses the *Rah-Rah* approach very well in some cases. I've personally seen a multi-level marketing company fill McCormick Place in Chicago, and bring the crowd of mostly new recruits to a near fever pitch. Maintaining that enthusiasm is more challenging.

◆　◆　◆

Most sales techniques require asking for the sale at some point. Once you ask for the sale, SHUT UP! The generally accepted rule is that the first one to speak loses. If the prospect speaks first, they have to buy, or express an objection or excuse. If the sales person

102

speaks first, the prospect is now off the hook.

If you haven't been in sales and aren't aware of this, test it. Once the closing question is asked, a good salesman will wait for you to respond. Test him or her. Don't talk. The quiet can seem eternal.

On several occasions, I've been out with salespeople in the field, when they can't stand the quiet after asking for the sale. If the prospect doesn't respond quickly, they start selling again. They may bring up new features and benefits, or repeat features and benefits that have already been mentioned. Keeping quiet can be a very hard lesson for some salespeople.

At one time in my career, I sold real estate franchises. Real estate franchises are normally called conversion franchises because they're generally sold to existing, independent real estate offices. I once called on a real estate broker who had several offices in his part of the state. He had already become the largest broker in his part of the state and wanted to get bigger.

After I'd made a presentation in his office, the next step of the sales process was to invite him to our regional office and training facilities for a more detailed presentation. He pointed out that he already had the largest real estate operation in that part of the state, and intended to get bigger.

He asked me why he needed a franchise. I responded, "You're the biggest now, but you want to get bigger. You have to decide if you can do it on your own, or if you can do it better with the help of a franchise." I then shut up and waited for a response.

It seemed like an eternity as I waited. This was a big sale for me at the time. I had just bought a new house and I needed the commission for the down payment. In my mind, I could see the dollar signs disappearing. It took all my will power to keep quiet and wait for a response.

It seemed like about a week later when he responded. He asked me when I wanted him to come in for a presentation at our regional offices and training facilities. That's the last time I had to ask a closing question. He converted all his offices to the franchise.

A twist on the closing questions is to phrase the question so the prospect must respond affirmative or talk to you. I will again use an example from when I sold real estate conversion franchises.

After the prospect had come into the regional office to meet the staff and see the regional office and training facility, I would then ask if they were ready to join the franchise. They never were and never brought a check along.

I would then make an appointment to come to their office in a few days with the franchise agreements to get a check and their signature. We were originally taught to not take any calls from the prospect until we saw them in their office. I found this forced the prospect into a *Yes* or *No* situation. If they were undecided, it tended to make them defensive and push them to *No*.

I didn't like this, so I changed the close slightly. I made the appointment in the prospect's office. I then said, "You understand that I'm coming to get the franchise agreements signed and pick up a check. If you have any problems with that, give me a call. I'm not driving over there for fun."

I'd now put them into a *Yes* or *Talk to me* situation. I liked that better. I had one prospect call me before I went to pick up his check and signature. I expected some objection or excuse. He just said that if I could get him into the next training class he would arrive a half hour early to sign the franchise agreement and give me a check.

I knew my prospect was a very well qualified Realtor. He'd already been approved for the franchise. I agreed and got him into the next training class. He'd just saved me a trip and a day.

My Regional Director said I shouldn't do it that way. I asked him why, as I handed him the check and signed agreements. My prospect was already in training.

There is one alternative to asking a closing question. That's the assumptive sale. The assumptive sale is just that. The sales person acts as if the prospect has already agreed to the sale. The salesperson is now just completing the details.

I once was involved with a construction company. I made a call on a prospect for a new office building. One of our company architects accompanied me. I used an assumptive close. After a short meeting, we left with a signed agreement to design the new office building.

When we got back in the car, the architect asked, "What just happened in there? I've always heard you have to ask for the sale." Obviously, the assumptive sale worked well in that specific situation. Sometimes the prospect even says, "What just happened?"

◆   ◆   ◆

Most sales systems are combinations of several techniques mentioned. Some are one-call or one-chance situations. Some involve many calls and a lot of tenacity. Some require a sales person that can handle a lot of rejection.

In most door-to-door sales and telephone marketing there is no second chance. The sales person must close the sale on the first call or there is no sale.

This is generally assumed to be true in the retail automobile business. A person that has to "think about it" and leaves is called a *Be Back*. Most retail automobile sales people say a *Be Back* is worth nothing, as most people will never come back. I don't totally agree with this, if a good rapport has been established.

In telemarketing, the telemarketer must be able to handle a lot of rejection, as most people will not even talk to them. The no-call lists have made this even harder, but by no means stop the telemarketing industry.

Most sales systems use a variety of techniques, and require a lot of tenacity to follow the system. When I worked in the recreational vehicle industry, I started as a sales manager for one of the company plants. We considered eight states to be our marketing area. I developed a detailed marketing plan with a detailed sales strategy. The strategy was quite simple and basically just a consistent follow-up system.

Some sales managers like the *Rah-Rah* approach for managing their sales people, as well as a sales technique for their salespeople to use on their prospects. This always turned me off personally.

After I took over the position of Plant Manager, I named one of my salesmen as sales manager. He followed my system and did quite well. One of our competitors tried to hire my sales manager. We had a good open relationship, and he told me about the offer. It was a good offer and I recommended he take it. He refused the offer. When I asked him why, he said that he liked the sales system I had developed and did not want to leave it.

◆ ◆ ◆

An essential part of any sales approach is prospecting. All sales approaches need prospects. If finding prospects is your responsibility, you must work that part of the system every day. Even if prospects are supplied to you, you should always be asking for referrals.

One of my sons, Aaron, had a job selling training seminars over the phone while in law school. For compensation he received a minimal salary plus commission and bonus. Aaron's training instructed him to always talk to the person in charge. They told him not to waste his time talking to anyone other than the person in charge.

Aaron told me this when he came home for a visit and was quite surprised when I responded with "Bull.". I told him to talk to the receptionist, secretary, or administrative assistant he got on the phone. This person knows who does what in the company and who the real decision makers are in the company. It may not be the owner, chief executive officer, chief operating officer, or even the department head.

Aaron took my advice and did quite well in the

job. He learned to use the receptionists, secretaries, and administrative assistants for his market research. He quickly learned how important a role an administrative assistant plays in any organization. Some administrative assistants have more time with an organization than most of the top management. In some cases, they might have *trained* several bosses.

One of the roles of an administrative assistant is to protect their boss, and their boss's time. In order to do this effectively, they must know who does what in the organization. Aaron quickly learned that the administrative assistant could tell him whom he should be talking to about the training seminars he offered.

With the help of the administrative assistants, Aaron could map out the company's organization chart with actual names. After identifying the potential buyer for the seminar he sold, Aaron could talk to them about features and benefits of the seminar. Aaron could also refer to other people in the organization by name, thus adding to his credibility. Aaron would be referring to people by name that he'd never talked with personally.

Aaron and I were talking on the phone one day while he was at work. Someone interrupted our call to tell him a secretary on the east coast was calling about someone he needed to talk to about some seminars. The call resulted in a sale. If Aaron had not *wasted* his time getting to know this secretary, he never would have known she had her finger on the pulse of the company. He never would have told her what he did, and he never would have gotten the sale.

Aaron became a top producer and got promoted to

management as a part-time employee and a full-time law student. He recently told me he had fun at the job and he could have made a career in sales if law school hadn't worked out.

◆ ◆ ◆

It's easy to get so busy with active prospects, that you stop searching for new prospects. If you fall into this trap, you'll wake up one day without a single prospect. Your sales will reflect this with radical highs and lows.

If you want consistent sales, you must be consistent with all facets of marketing including prospecting. You must always be marketing, and not stop because sales are good. Sales won't stay that way without marketing.

Your prospecting activities may be weekly, or daily, but they must be on a regular schedule. Being too busy is no excuse for not prospecting. If you do, you'll wake up one day with no clients and no new prospects.

Successful sales are both an art and a science. For consistent sales results, a good plan must be developed and worked every day. As the old saying goes, "Plan your work and work your plan."

Chapter 15: Independent Contractors

We probably need to discuss what an independent contractor is and how it can affect your business. An independent contractor is *not an employee*. There are over twenty legal conditions that define an independent contractor verses an employee. These guidelines may also change slightly from one state to another.

A very general description of an independent contractor is someone who performs some service for another individual or company and is compensated in some way other than a salary or hourly wage. The independent contractor may provide sales and be compensated by commission. An independent contractor may also provide a service other than sales and be compensated on a per-job or per-piece basis.

Independent contractors are free to perform the service when, where, and how they want. No workplace is provided. The independent contractor sets his or her own hours. They are free to perform the job in any manner they wish.

An independent contractor will receive a 1099 showing how much they were paid over the previous year. There will be no taxes withheld. Taxes are the responsibility of the independent contractor, who is self-employed.

With an employer-employee relationship, the employer is responsible for withholding taxes and social security from the employee's compensation. The employer will give a W-2 to the employee at the end of the year. The employer may also provide the employee with other benefits, such as paid vacations and holidays, sick leave, and medical insurance.

You may wish to use independent contractors in your business. Be very careful that the relationship with your independent contractors meets all the legal requirements so no one can determine they are actually employees. This can create problems for you with the IRS and your state department of revenue. It can also create other legal liabilities.

◆ ◆ ◆

Here are some general guidelines for determining whether or not an individual is an employee:

- An employee is told how and when the work is to be done.

- The work is performed at the company's place of business or a place provided by the company.

- The employer sets the work schedule.

- The work must not be contracted to another party.

- They are paid hourly, weekly, or monthly as opposed to totally commission or by the job.

- The work provided is done exclusively for one company versus several companies.

- The worker is required to devote full-time or a defined part-time effort to the job.

- Regular oral or written reports are required.

- There is a continuing relationship.

- The worker is subject to dismissal for reasons other than non-performance under the contract.

- The worker can terminate the relationship without incurring any liability for failure to complete a job.

- Business and travel expenses are reimbursed.

- Services provided by the worker are integral to company's operations.

- The company hires, supervises, or pays assistants for the worker.

- The employee is provided training to perform a job in a particular method or manner.

- The company furnishes tools and materials used by the worker.

- The worker has no investment in tools or equipment to provide the service.

- The worker does not have a chance of realizing a loss under the relationship.

◆ ◆ ◆

This is a general list of conditions defining an employee. It is not intended to be a complete list. Specifics may vary by laws of the federal government, the IRS, and individual states.

If any of these conditions exist, the individual probably will be considered an employee and not an independent contractor. All of these conditions may not need to be applicable for an individual to be considered an employee. An individual might be considered an employee with only one condition existing.

Some companies pay their employees on a commission or bonus basis and maintain the control of an employer/employee relationship. They do this by simply guaranteeing the employee some minimum wage. Obviously, the employee that doesn't produce at some minimum level will be terminated.

◆ ◆ ◆

I once worked as a director of marketing for a company that used independent contractors for some of its sales. I was very careful to meet all the criteria to insure these individuals would not be considered employees. We didn't provide any place for them to work. We didn't tell them when to work. We didn't tell them how or where to produce the sales. We gave them no exclusivity for any area. We compensated on a percentage for those sales they produced. Our attorney said we had the cleanest independent contractor relationship he'd ever seen. We met all the legal requirements of an independent contractor relationship.

Unfortunately, one of our independent contractors wasn't very successful in the business. His previous career had been in automobile sales and he wasn't able to schedule his own time and make the big-ticket sale we'd contracted with him to produce. He became disgruntled over a *house deal*, or a sale made by company staff and employees. The independent contractor had nothing to do with the sale. The sale was in a geographic area he considered his area in spite

113

of the fact that he had no geographic responsibility or exclusivity.

Now keep in mind that this individual had absolutely nothing coming, as he hadn't been involved in the sale and had earned no commission. He threatened to sue us, and I offered him what I considered a generous settlement to have him go away.

He wasn't happy with what I offered him and took us to court. His attorney asked for a jury trial. His attorney made sure no one on the jury had ever been an independent contractor, or had ever been in business for themselves, or had ever been in sales. In other words, no one on the jury had any concept of how any type of commissioned sales worked.

The trial lasted three days. As director of marketing, I sat on the witness stand for over twelve hours. We made a good case. We impeached the plaintiff on several points.

In spite of the fact the plaintiff had nothing to do with the sale and lied on the stand, the jury awarded him $30,000. They also called him an employee. Calling him an employee in that state meant that any judgment automatically doubled by state statute. This increased the award to $60,000. The law also allowed attorney fees on top of the settlement. Since the plaintiff's attorney received one third of the total settlement, our total cost reached $90,000 plus our attorney fees. This amounted to a lot of money in 1980.

The decision was a joke, and we thought the judge might throw it out. After consideration, he let the jury's award stand.

We appealed the decision to the state supreme court. The state supreme court ruled that the decision was a travesty of justice, but since the trial had broken no rule of law, nothing could be done about it.

Be careful if you use independent contractors in your business. They can be an effective tool, but don't put controls on them so they might be considered employees.

Chapter 16: Advertising

The first things that typically come to mind when people think of marketing are sales and advertising. We've already devoted a whole chapter to sales, so now let's talk about advertising.

The advantage of media advertising is it provides for significant exposure at a relatively low cost per exposure. The disadvantage is that there is not as much control over who sees the advertisement. Other marketing tools may be better targeted at specific prospects.

When we think of advertising, we often think about television advertising. Most of us watch TV and are exposed to advertising on a regular basis.

A 30-second ad on the Super Bowl will not fit most of our marketing plans with a cost of $3,000,000 or more, plus production costs. That media may work for Budweiser, but won't fit most of our budgets. Television advertising is generally perceived as expensive. Network advertisements that run nationally are very expensive.

You can also buy ads in local television markets. These ads cost considerably less than ads with national exposure. The viewing area for a TV station is called its Designated Market Area or DMA. If you're an old fart like me, you may remember this as an ADI, or Area of Dominant Influence.

Cable networks have also changed television

advertising. An advertisement on a local cable channel may well fit your budget. This may be the best buy for you, but remember, one ad will not do the job.

If you're selling golf equipment, a golf channel makes sense because you'll have less waste coverage. A national ad on a golf channel for a local golf course would have too much waste coverage. Waste coverage is anyone seeing your advertisement that's not a potential customer for your product or service.

◆ ◆ ◆

The next advertising media to think of is radio. Radio normally costs less than television. Be careful to check who the audience is for any station you consider. It doesn't matter what the cost is or how many people are being reached if they aren't your potential customers.

Buying time on a rap station is probably not a good buy if you're marketing services for the aging or baby boomers. A rap station doesn't appeal to many of your aging potential customers.

◆ ◆ ◆

Print is the next advertising media I'll mention. Major newspapers may reach the most people per dollar. Some newspapers now have national coverage. This may be great if your customers are widespread. If your customers are all concentrated in a ten-mile area, everything outside this ten-mile area is wasted coverage and wasted advertising dollars.

Newspaper is the most common print media used by small businesses. A local paper may fit your needs the best. It may fit the geographic area you serve.

If you're located in a large metro area, the major

newspaper may have too much waste coverage for your business. Remember the individual I mentioned who started a lawn mowing business in the Minneapolis-Saint Paul area. The major newspaper produced prospects over too large an area for him to service efficiently. A neighborhood paper or other marketing tools would have been a much better choice to promote his business.

You have two ways to advertise in a newspaper. You can run display ads or classified ads. You must determine which produces the results you want. Track the results so you know where to invest your marketing dollars.

Writing an effective ad is essential to producing good results. Buying media space does no good if the copy doesn't attract your potential customer. The media may have writers available for little or no charge, or you may want to hire a professional writer.

Always look for ways to get free publicity in the newspaper. This can be more effective than advertisements. Plus, the price is better.

◆　◆　◆

One of my sons was born during my time as a Ford Mercury dealer in a small Midwest town. When Aaron reached about a year old, the editor of the local newspaper kept bugging me to use Aaron in my ads.

I finally agreed and we ran an ad campaign one fall in conjunction with a promotion to give away some stadium kits with the purchase of a car. The ad showed a large picture of Aaron sitting on a stadium blanket on the hood of a car. He was holding a Thermos with the rest of the stadium kit next to him.

The copy simply said:

Hi, I'm Aaron Lee.

I love my daddy.

You'll love the deals my daddy is making on new 1974 cars & pickups. And he is giving away all this stuff with every new car.

Stadium kit includes insulated bag, 1 qt. Thermos, and 100% acrylic fiber blanket.

Everyone in town knew Aaron. We got a lot of calls and compliments on the ads. And, most importantly, the ads achieved their purpose. We sold cars.

◆   ◆   ◆

Magazine advertising can be an effective media for your business, because it targets specific groups of people. This might mean you have less waste coverage. Using golf as an example again, a golf magazine might be a very good media if you're are selling golf equipment.

Buying an ad in a golf magazine with national distribution might result in a lot of waste coverage if you're promoting a local golf course. Check with the magazine to see if you can buy an ad for only those magazines distributed in your area. A regional edition may be an option.

Another option that can save money is buying

Remnants. Remnants are unsold space in a magazine. If one fourth of a page is not sold, the magazine will sell that space for a greatly reduced price.

Jay Conrad Levinson proposes some interesting twists with magazine advertising in his book *Guerrilla Marketing.* He suggests running a full page, four-color ad one time and then using reprints of that ad in other ways like a flyer or poster.

Levinson also suggests referencing the magazine ad in other marketing efforts to promote the image. Lines like "As seen in Good Housekeeping" can promote a quality image.

◆ ◆ ◆

Yellow page advertising can be essential to your business, or a total waste of money. This is a decision you must make. Does your potential customer look in the yellow pages for your product or service? If not, a standard listing with no display ad is sufficient. Don't spend money on yellow page advertising *just because.* Do your research.

Yellow page advertising isn't cheap and there may be several directories serving any given area. There are at least four where I live. Do you need to be in all of them? Many people feel that if you do need a display ad in the yellow pages, you need an ad as big as your competition.

Yellow page advertising is an essential part of the marketing program in some industries. It is so important in some industries that some franchises want new franchisees to start their operations timed to when the new yellow pages come out with their full-page advertisements.

♦ ♦ ♦

Outdoor advertising can be a great marketing tool. In the *olden days*, outdoor advertising was creative and varied. People put signs on fence posts and painted signs on barns as well as more conventional billboards.

Most of you are probably too young to remember two of my personal favorite outdoor advertising campaigns. They are Burma-Shave and Wall Drug.

Burma-Shave is considered a pioneer in brushless shaving. Burma-Shave spent their entire advertising budget on outdoor advertising. They used a series of six roadside signs positioned on fence posts with an appropriate spacing so they could easily be read by passing motorists. The signs were always red with white letters, and the last sign always said Burma-Shave.

Those were the days of two lane highways, before interstates. It was hard for a motorist to resist reading the signs unless they were read aloud by a passenger.

Sometimes Burma-Shave signs promoted a clean shave like in this example. (1) His cheek (2) Was rough (3) His chick vamoosed (4) And now she won't (5) Come home to roost (6) Burma-Shave

Sometimes the signs urged motorists to drive carefully like in this example. (1) The place to pass (2) On curves (3) You know (4) Is only at (5) A beauty show (6) Burma-Shave.

A large portion of the Burma-Shave factory was devoted to producing the roadside signs. Burma-Shave had full-time employees traveling the country installing the signs.

♦ ♦ ♦

As I mentioned, I grew up on a farm in northern Iowa. When I was about ten years old my family took a vacation. We drove to South Dakota and Wyoming. We planned on seeing the Black Hills, the Badlands National Park, Mount Rushmore, and Yellowstone National Park. What did I want to see? Old Faithful and Mount Rushmore sounded okay, but seeing Wall Drug is what really excited me.

Wall Drug is a store in Wall, South Dakota near the Badlands National Park. Ted and Dorothy Hustead bought the drug store in 1931, before the completion of Mount Rushmore.

They struggled to make a living for five years. In the summer of 1936 Dorothy realized that the people traveling on the nearby highways were hot and dusty. They really wanted ice water.

They made up some signs for free ice water. They copied Burma-Shave. The original signs read; (1) Get a Soda (2) Get a root beer (3) Turn next corner (4) Just as near (5) To Highway 16 & 14 (6) Free Ice Water (7) Wall Drug. By the next summer, Wall Drug had added eight employees.

Wall Drug expanded their highway signs all over the country. Most of these signs were just small signs that said how many miles to Wall Drug. There were several close to where we lived in Iowa. I saw them frequently. One said, "Only 451 miles to Wall Drug."

Wall Drug became a popular tourist attraction. They're not far off I-90. They still promote free ice water. Wall Drug is still visited by as many as 20,000 people on a summer day.

Regulations and environmentalists today prevent

highway signs like Burma-Shave and Wall Drug used. Today, we are restricted to the more structured highway signs and billboards.

Outdoor signs can be simple or very elaborate. A big advantage, or disadvantage, to outdoor advertising is that the sign is location specific. If the people you want to reach are passing by this location, the right people will see the sign.

Price will vary depending on the size, type, location, and traffic count for the sign. Do you need a sign that is lighted or illuminated at night? You can own your sign or rent the space by the month.

◆ ◆ ◆

One common tool in advertising is promoting a *Loss Leader*. This is quite simply selling one or more products at a very attractive price to get people into your place of business. You may even sell these items at below cost as the term *Loss Leader* implies.

This is a legal and often effective marketing tool. You will want to locate the loss leader item somewhere in your store where the customer will see and buy something else while in the store. Loss leader items are often located in the back of the store. If you only sell the item you are losing money with, the promotion is not doing you any good.

The *Loss Leader* is totally different than a *Bait and Switch,* which is illegal. I obviously do not recommend using *Bait and Switch* advertising that is illegal, but very hard to prove and prosecute.

In the car business, a common *Bait and Switch* is the practice of advertising a stripped down model at a low price and then having the sales person move the customer up to a higher priced model with a higher profit margin. This practice is common in the car business and many other industries.

As a Ford-Mercury dealer, I saw an ad for a stripped down Ford pickup in my state at a price I calculated to be at, or below, cost. I saw the dealer who had run the ad at a meeting and asked him if he actually had that stripped down pickup in stock. He responded, "I have *one* in stock, and the sales person that sells it is fired, and they all know it."

◆ ◆ ◆

When planning a media advertising campaign, remember, one ad will normally not do the job. One TV or radio ad will not make a successful campaign. One print ad will not make a successful campaign. It will take more than one. It may take using a mix of several media.

I had a marketing professor once tell me that with print advertising, a potential customer may *see* the ad the first time, *read* the ad the second time, and *remember* the ad the third time. Your potential customer will also not be exposed to every ad you run, so it will take more than three to expose the potential customer three times.

Most advertising promoting a brand or name does not work overnight. The Marlboro man is one of the most successful cigarette ad campaigns ever, but it didn't work overnight. The Leo Burnett Advertising Agency created the campaign for Phillip Morris in 1954. They didn't see an increase in sales the first year, but they stuck with the campaign. By 1972 Marlboro was the #1 cigarette brand. The ad campaign became so successful that it ran for forty-six years from 1954 to 1999.

When you have a good marketing campaign, stick with it. It's tempting to change when you, your employees, and especially your sales people get tired of it. Your customer is probably just starting to identify with you, your campaign, and your product or service.

Chapter 17: Promotion

There are many marketing and promotion tools besides traditional advertising. Let's take a look at a few.

Direct mail is a very good option for many businesses. The cost for direct mail will be higher per customer reached than most media, but there are advantages.

Your direct mail piece can be a personal letter. You can target direct mail to specific geographic areas. You may be able to target specific customer profiles.

The life of a direct mail piece may be longer than other advertising media. If the direct mail piece is of interest to the prospective customer, they may save it and not throw it out with yesterday's paper.

◆ ◆ ◆

When I started Collectible Car Showcase in the Chicago-land area, I did a large and relatively expensive mailing. I purchased the subscription lists for the Chicago-land area from two magazines targeting the collectible car buff. I then merged these two lists to prevent duplication.

I mailed a letter introducing Collectible Car Showcase. I also included a two-color, three-fold brochure. I normally don't recommend including brochures in mailings, as this increases the cost. It's usually better to let the prospect request the brochure.

In this case, I felt the mailing list had so little

waste coverage that it justified the cost. We had a very high and successful initial response.

The mailing also had and excellent *life*, as many people saved the brochure. Collectible Car Showcase continued getting calls from people who had saved the brochure a year later.

◆　◆　◆

The telephone may be a great marketing tool. We first think of telemarketing, which seems to be thriving in spite of the *No Call* lists. A good call list is an important part of any telemarketing program.

In my opinion, the telephone is most effective once potential customers have been identified. I attended an entrepreneurial club meeting once when a couple that produced *buttons* approached me about the right kind of advertising media for them.

They produced the type of buttons that carried a message like "Vote for Bush." Almost all of their buttons were custom orders. When I asked who ordered their buttons, they said almost all their sales went to advertising specialty companies.

I asked if they could easily identify these advertising specialty companies. When they said yes, I suggested a structured and tenacious telephone campaign targeting advertising specialty companies.

◆　◆　◆

As sales manager for the recreational vehicle manufacturer, we marketed to recreational vehicle dealers in an eight state area. When I went to work for the company as sales manager we had about thirty semi-active dealers. I contacted these dealers and started to physically identify the other dealers we wanted. Once I'd identified the dealers I wanted, I started a structured phone campaign.

I spent every Monday in the office making calls to dealers. I called current and prospective dealers. I called a dealer every week, every two weeks, or every four weeks, depending on the size of the dealer. The largest dealers received a call every week and the smallest dealers every four weeks.

When I contacted them, I didn't normally try to sell them anything. I just said, "This is Terry Lee from Compliment. I'm just calling to see if there is anything I can do for you." My approach relied on the idea that eventually their existing suppliers would mess up and they would give us a chance.

Compliment was our brand name, not our company name. I felt the prospective dealers would identify with our brand name more than with our company name. The brand name is what I promoted, and hopefully what the dealer would eventually be selling.

After eight months, we had gone from thirty dealers to one hundred and sixty. We went from selling forty units a month when I started as sales manager to selling forty units a day. Now we had a production problem instead of a sales problem, because the plant only produced twenty units per day, half as many as we were selling; but that is another story.

◆　◆　◆

The Internet now offers a wide variety of options to advertise and market your goods and services. You may want to have your own web site. If you do, you'll want to list that site in all your marketing materials.

Don't make the mistake of thinking once you have your own web site, customers will flock to you. Your potential customers will have to find your web site. You'll need to learn about *search engines*. Once people find your site, the site must motivate them to take some action.

The best web site in the world alone will not make you a success. It's just one part of your marketing plan. It's an electronic brochure and nothing more. Too many new businesses make the mistake of thinking a web site is their total marketing plan and it's all they need. Wrong. Big mistake. You must promote your web site with all the other marketing tools you're using.

You can market your products on sites like E-bay, Craigslist, and Amazon. You can also advertise on other sites with ads or pop-ups. You may be able to buy prospects on a per-prospect basis. You can often find sites that will let you advertise for free.

I feel e-mail is one of the most important tools of the Internet. This is a form of direct mail that can be very cost effective when compared to traditional snail mail. The most important part of an effective e-mail marketing program is developing a good e-mail mailing list. This part is just the same as traditional direct mail.

Other opportunities the Internet offers are blogs, tweets, Facebook, pod casting, and nanocasting. The Internet is constantly changing as a marketing tool. It's becoming a more and more important part of any marketing plan. I won't attempt to address the Internet in any detail.

As with most things, using these tools effectively will require time and effort. I have a blog called *Common Sense, Business & Politics*. The blog address is terryoliverlee.blogspot.com. I try to post a new blog at least once a week, but it takes time, effort, and organization to be effective. If you start a blog and only post to it occasionally, it won't be effective.

Unless you're very familiar with all the options the Internet offers for marketing, it may be a little overwhelming. I know it is for an *old fart* like me. You may need professional help in this area. This help may not be cheap, but may be more cost effective in the long run. Do your research. Don't make the mistake of thinking that just having your own web site will solve all your marketing problems. That is as crazy as, "Build a better mouse trap and customers will beat a path to your door."

◆　◆　◆

When I was general manager of Duffy's Collectible Cars, we were the clear leader in the collectible car industry. On average we bought and sold a collectible car every day.

During this time, the Internet was just becoming a significant media for buying and selling collector cars. Several magazines devoted to advertising collectible cars started web sites for selling collector cars. They asked me to put our inventory on their web site for free simply because of our position in the industry, and they wanted to show an inventory of nice collectible cars for sale. I agreed, but I started our own web site at the same time.

These web sites wanted to show the large

inventory, and I added new listings weekly as the individual sites requested. The problem was that they continued to list sold vehicles for months after they were sold. Potential customers often became irritated when they called on a specific car only to find out it had been sold.

They were very nice web sites and the magazines did a good job promoting them, but they didn't keep the sites current. I eventually demanded that our entire inventory be removed from those sites.

This is typical for new web sites. The entire budget is spent on developing the site. Without promotion and maintenance, the money to develop it in the first place may be wasted.

We developed our own web site. We promoted the site in all our advertising and brochures. We faithfully maintained it and updated the inventory every week.

We soon had so many hits that people were trying to buy advertising on our site. One of our administrators for the site said we could make a lot of money by selling ad spots. Right or wrong, we decided to keep the site exclusive and not sell outside advertising.

Our first two years advertising collectible cars on the Internet were not very productive. We credited the Internet for two cars sold from that media during that time. In the fifth year of our own web site, the site accounted for over twenty percent of our sales. Don't give up if results are not immediate.

◆ ◆ ◆

Are you going to have a brochure? A brochure can be anything from a standard 8½ x 11 piece of paper that's folded three times, to a small book. It can be plain black and white to four-color. Obviously, the price varies drastically.

We've have already talked about web sites as an electronic brochure. You may need both electronic and print brochures, or just one, or neither. It depends on your product or service, and your total marketing plan. You should also consider CDs and DVDs.

Production and per piece costs will vary drastically. With some options the initial production cost is high and the cost per piece is low. Sometimes it's the opposite. You'll have to determine how you're going to use the brochure and how many you'll need. As the price goes up, you must be more selective about how you use them.

◆　◆　◆

The circular or flyer can also be very effective marketing tools. The cost for these can be quite low if ordered in volume, or by using your own equipment.

A flyer or circular can be as simple as black ink on white paper. It may be color ink or color paper, but it should always be limited to a single sheet of paper. It may be the four-color reprint of the magazine ad mentioned earlier.

Flyers or circulars can be distributed in many ways, and any place you're in contact with potential customers. They can be handed out on the sidewalk or in a mall. They can be posted on bulletin boards. Flyers or circulars can be put under windshield wipers.

Flyers can be put in doors. A variation of the circular or flyer is the *Door Hanger*. The door hanger can be a very effective marketing tool when targeting a small geographic market.

Remember the individual I mentioned who started a mowing business? He took out an ad in the large metro newspaper. Door hangers would have been a much better marketing investment.

He could have concentrated his marketing in a compact area that he could effectively and economically service. When he serviced an existing customer, door hangers should have been left with the neighbors of that customer.

◆ ◆ ◆

Another effective marketing tool is a business card. The business card must contain some basic information. Your business card should promote the product or service you offer.

Some business cards have photos, logos, or graphics. The cost of the card goes up of course. I do recommend you keep your business card a standard size that fits in a card file or it may get thrown away. You may want to print something on the back of the card, but it should not be any of the essential information.

Some business cards are folded so they can contain more information. I am not a big fan of this as the cost goes up, and only one side is visible in a card file anyway. The most relevant information must be on the front of the business card so it's visible in a card file.

Business cards can be displayed on desks, counters, and bulletin boards. They may be considered an inexpensive flyer or brochure. I've known people who had such expensive business cards that they tried to qualify and control who got one. This is stupid. Make your business card available to anyone who might be a potential customer.

◆ ◆ ◆

Point-of-purchase signs can be as effective as another sales clerk if used properly. Remember, a high percentage of buying decisions are impulse buys. Point-of-purchase signs are such an important part of retailing that they make up a significant portion of most sign company's business.

In the days of the large department stores in the downtown areas of our cities, window displays were an important part of their marketing strategy. With the high foot traffic past the stores, window displays were designed to draw people into the store. These displays can be a very effective marketing tool.

Outside displays can also be an effective marketing tool. In the car business, a vehicle might be called *Front Row Ready*. This normally refers to a used vehicle that would draw in customers if placed in a highly visible spot in the front row.

One time in the Ford-Mercury dealership, I bought a current year, bright red, Chevrolet Vega at auction. The car looked good and was *Front Row Ready*. I eventually sold the Vega at a loss, but the Vega made me a lot of money. Here's how.

The car looked good on the front row of my used car lot. It drew customers who were considering buying a new Vega as an economy car. I instructed my sales people to get the customer to also drive a new Ford Pinto or Mercury Bobcat.

The Vega was always for sale and the sales person

would sell it to anyone who wanted it, so it was not a *Bait and Switch* as we discussed in the advertising chapter. Since the Pinto and Bobcat were superior vehicles to the Vega, we sold a lot of Pintos and Bobcats.

◆ ◆ ◆

Gift certificates can be a great marketing tool. They should be promoted in all advertising, but especially with point-of-purchase signs. Some retailers now give a free gift card with the purchase of a gift card. Giving a free $5 gift card with the purchase of a $20 gift card may be a good incentive. The buyer of the gift card can keep the $5 gift card or give it away.

Because gift cards are getting some bad publicity now, I wouldn't recommend putting an expiration date on the card, or any other restrictions. If you do have restrictions on where or how the gift card must be used, make them very clear.

We once gave a gift card for a food franchise to some friends in another state. This particular food franchise used regional developers, which we'll discuss later. These regional developers didn't honor gift cards from outside their region. This is a big mistake for the franchise, in my opinion. It proved an embarrassment for us, and the people to whom we gave the gift cards.

◆ ◆ ◆

A coupon can be a good marketing tool. Part of the public loves coupons. I know of at least one franchise in a specific industry that is almost totally coupon driven.

Amazingly, the price isn't as important in some businesses as is the discount available through a coupon. For example, most people in the retail pizza business feel they get more business with the use of coupons than if they just lowered the price.

One marketing strategy may be to keep the price high and use coupons to discount the price. This gives the consumer a perception of both quality and value.

When I started an automotive service franchise, we used direct mail companies like Money Mailer or Valpak. We mailed coupons with these direct mail companies. The coupons brought new customers into our business.

The coupons were also used by previous customers, and got them back to our business. The coupons were a reward for these customers to be repeat customers. Remember, marketing should be for both present and potential customers.

◆　◆　◆

Advertising specialty items, promotional items, and giveaways are all excellent marketing tools if used properly. So, be careful with these. Remember, the object is to make a profit, not to give it away. For example, a refrigerator magnet that's thrown in the garbage is wasted profit.

At the Ford-Mercury dealership, I once offered to sell kids a very nice coaster wagon with removable sideboards for one cent when their parents bought a new or used car. Obviously, one of the keys to the promotion was making kids aware of the coaster wagons for a penny. The coaster wagons cost us money, but when kids heard their parents mention a new or different car, they begged their parents to go to Lee Motors. Once the parents were in the dealership and the kids saw the coaster wagons, we had a good chance to make the sale.

◆　◆　◆

I did another very successful giveaway at the car dealership. I gave away free motor oil for the life of the car with the purchase of any new car. This offer was only good for the original owner. We made this strictly a verbal agreement with nothing in writing. Motor oil changes were recommended every 3,000 to 5,000 miles.

The motor oil was free, but we charged a small lubrication fee and we charged for the oil filter. Every oil change required both. For those of you not familiar with cars of the early 70's and before, steering components back then had grease zerks requiring grease for lubrication as part of the regularly scheduled maintenance.

We used only recommended Ford oil filters and Ford motor oil from bulk. We always explained the terms and conditions clearly to the customer.

If a car used any oil between changes, we would give the owner free quarts of oil to take with them. Great for customer relations, as nobody liked their new car to use oil. Many cars from that time period used some oil and Ford wouldn't do an engine tear-down unless it used more than one quart every 700 miles.

The sales force loved the promotion as it gave them something to distinguish Lee Motors from our competition. Our customers loved the *Free Motor Oil* promotion.

The promotion worked well as it helped sell cars and trucks. We still made money on every oil change, plus we had the vehicle back in the shop for any additional service work needed.

The give-away made money all the way around. Our customers, sales staff, and service staff all loved the giveaway. I never understood why our competition didn't match our offer.

◆ ◆ ◆

Word-of-mouth advertising and networking are probably some of the most effective marketing tools available. I have a handy man we'll call Steve. Steve got fed up with his construction job and the traffic in the Twin Cities.

Steve started a one-man business called The Simple Guy Property Services. He wanted to keep the business simple, and he didn't want any employees. He started the business with a pickup and tools he already owned.

Steve initially marketed his business by posting business cards on bulletin boards in the area. Steve's a nice guy who did what he said when he said. If there were any problems, he called the customer and told them. He did good work at a fair price. Word-of-mouth and repeat business did the rest.

Steve now has all the work he wants, and he handpicks those jobs. He no longer posts his business cards on the bulletin boards. Steve's concerned he'll be too busy during the winter, and not have enough time for ice fishing, his favorite activity.

Does this sound simple? Yes and no. Steve did his homework. He determined the service he would provide and how he'd provide it. He identified his customer. He priced his service. He picked a name that gave the image he wanted. He designed a good business card. He consistently posted these business cards on bulletin boards in his identified market area.

The rest was easy, but somewhat unusual. He did what he said when he said, and he talked to the customer. If there were any problems, he communicated with his customer. He did good work at a fair price. I repeat. He did what he said when he said. This doesn't sound too hard, but amazingly is somewhat unusual in the construction business.

◆ ◆ ◆

Networking can be an important part of marketing. We all have a circle of influence and come in contact with people every day. Interaction with these people can be effective marketing that will generate business. Networking is a great way to meet new prospects and get referrals.

Networking is important because people prefer to do business with people they know, like, and trust. You still have to offer your customer good value. Stay in touch.

You need to practice how to describe what you do in one minute or less. This is often referred to as an *Elevator Speech*, because it should be short enough to give in an elevator ride. Asking someone what he or she does is a common conversation starter. If asked, tell them, but keep it short.

You should also ensure your employees are able to give an elevator speech. Employees should be promoting the business to secure their own job. If an employee works in one small area of a company, they may not know what the company actually does. I've heard employees describe the company they work for incorrectly, or in an uncomplimentary manner. Train your employees on how to promote your business.

There are all kinds of ways to network. Being active in your community is a good start. Banks traditionally encourage their employees to be active in the community. They even encourage it on company time. They know these networking activities produce business.

Your local Chamber of Commerce could prove useful. Some Chambers have networking cocktail parties at member's businesses. One Chamber I belonged to called these events a PM Exchange. They held them once a month on a Thursday night from 5:00 to 7:00 p.m. They were great social and networking events. I found them enjoyable, and they brought me business.

Other events to consider would be service organizations like the Jaycees, Kiwanis, Lions, and Rotary. Being a guest speaker for these organizations might also be an opportunity to promote your business. Don't forget about youth organizations and your church.

There are also various business networking organizations including BNI. You know how I hate Acronyms, but BNI is the name. It probably originally stood for something like Business Networking International, but who knows. They claim to be the world's largest referral organization.

◆　◆　◆

Public relations or PR is not really promotion or advertising, but I'll address it here. Public relations is news that tells a story. An article in the paper about you, your company, your product, or service is public relations. I've heard public relations called free advertising. Public relations can also be more effective than a paid advertisement.

Research where and how you can get free public relations for your business. Learn how to write a good press release and where to send it. If this is not your forte, assign your public relations to someone else in your organization, or hire someone to handle it. It may be a good investment.

Chapter 18: Customer Service

Remember, my definition of marketing included present and potential customers. When we talked advertising and promotions we always kept both present and potential customers in mind. Most sales people say the best sales prospect is a past customer. This is true in most industries.

It's a lot easier to retain a customer than it is to attract a new customer. We should make every effort to keep our customers and keep them happy. Communication is the key. If you have a good rapport with a customer, the odds are you will have a satisfied and happy customer who will be a repeat customer.

Do what you do and do it well. This doesn't mean trying to be everything to everybody, as we discussed before. If a customer asks for something you don't provide, tell them. Maybe even refer the customer to someone that can meet the customer's needs. Communicate.

◆ ◆ ◆

When I took over as sales manager for the recreational vehicle plant, I inherited several problems. One major problem was customer service.

The plant manager showed me a stack of warranty claims from our dealers. All claims covered by our warranty had been paid, but none of these claims were covered under the company's warranty. The plant manager blamed the previous sales manager for not explaining the warranty, and no one had called the dealers to explain why the claims weren't covered under the warranty. There'd been absolutely no communication with these dealers.

Since nobody knew how to handle the claims, no one called the dealers back. The dealers were unhappy because they hadn't been reimbursed for the warranty claims, and no one had even bothered to call them.

I called every dealer and had the plant manager sit and listen with a muted phone. I told the dealer I was calling about his warranty claims. I then reviewed our warranty with him before going over each individual claim. We could then determine why the claim wasn't covered.

When I'd covered the claims for that dealer, the normal response was that they hadn't understood the warranty, and didn't feel they had anything coming. I apologized for the misunderstanding and lack of communication. I then told each dealer we would honor all the claims this time with the understanding that we would adhere to the terms of the warranty in the future.

I didn't give credit or discounts on future business; I cut checks to the dealers and mailed them the same day. This cost the company some money, but it bought us a lot of good will with our dealers.

Future warranty claims were processed the same day they were received. The dealer received a call informing them the claim had been received, and the check was being mailed that day. If we had any problem with the claim, we contacted the dealer the same day. Prompt communication is the most important thing with good customer service.

♦ ♦ ♦

The most important lesson in customer service is that when there is a problem, we must talk to that customer the same day. No exceptions. Prompt communication is essential.

I later took over as plant manager for the recreational vehicle plant. As I observed the various managers who had contact with dealers, I saw many pink phone messages from our dealers lying on their desks. When I asked why these phone calls hadn't been returned, they normally responded by saying they knew why the dealer was calling, and did not have an answer yet.

I explained that talking to the dealer the same day he called was more important than giving an answer to his question. I told them to let the dealer know they didn't have an answer yet, but would call the dealer back at some specific time. They needed to call the dealer back at that time, even if they still didn't have an answer.

This met with limited success. I didn't have time to give extensive training in customer service, so I told the individuals involved that all desks would be cleared of phone messages every night and wouldn't just be put in a drawer. People not adhering to this problem would be terminated.

Problem solved. Once implemented, both employees and dealers were happy with the policy. The irate dealer calls pretty much ended. Talking to the customer promptly is more important than the actual response.

The first rule of customer service is communication. The second rule is never lie to a customer. You will get caught, and you may never be able to correct this cardinal sin.

A good friend and business associate once told me he couldn't lie, because he wasn't smart enough to remember who he told what. One way or another you'll eventually get caught and lose a customer. That customer will tell another ten or twenty people, who you will also lose as customers or potential customers. Even liars hate a liar. If you're going to be in business, you cannot afford to lie.

Never promise the customer something you cannot deliver. If you don't deliver, the customer will interpret this as a lie. Always try to deliver more than you promise.

I've ordered things on the Internet that promised two to three week delivery. I often get this item in three to five days. The supplier knew delivery would be in three to five days if in stock and there were no problems, but they don't want the customer calling in three days so they say two to three weeks. They delivered more than they promised.

◆ ◆ ◆

In the recreational vehicle plant, we'd gotten very busy. We managed to meet all promised delivery times, but remained further out with deliveries than I liked. I had one dealer who always wanted special treatment and delivery yesterday. He also wanted delivery specifically on weekday mornings. This created some scheduling problems for us. The dealer was also very unfriendly to my drivers, and never provided adequate help for unloading.

One Friday afternoon, he called about his order, which had been promised for the following week. He wanted it today. I told him his order would arrive the following Monday morning. The dealer insisted he needed the order for the weekend. The dealer was only a few hours away.

I told the dealer I had a driver coming in who had been on the road for several days. I told him I would ask the driver to make a special trip to help the dealer out on the condition that the dealer took delivery later that night and kept enough help around to assist with the unloading.

I knew my driver would be willing to make the evening run. A couple hours later, I called the dealer and told him my driver was willing to make the evening delivery to help him out. I reminded the dealer to have help available for unloading.

When I saw my driver on Monday, he asked what I had done to that dealer. He said the dealer was not only friendly and had ample help for unloading, but also had fresh coffee and sandwiches waiting for him. We never had a problem scheduling deliveries with that dealer again.

Luckily, the dealer recognized we'd done him a favor, but be very careful about bending the rules or doing special favors for customers. It is my experience that the customer I give special service to is the one who usually bites me in the ass later.

◆　◆　◆

The second rule of customer service is to never lie to a customer, but this doesn't mean you can't have fun with customers. Car dealers don't always have the best reputation. This is a public perception, and usually not deserved.

It's more likely for the customer to lie to the sales person than the other way around. The sales person knows the damage a bad reputation can mean to his business. There are exceptions of course.

I once had a salesman with over twenty years of automobile experience walk into my office looking shocked. He explained he'd been watching the shop check out a car he'd just taken in on trade. I asked what was wrong with the car.

My salesman responded, "Nothing. It's just like they described it." He couldn't believe the honest description the customer had given for their trade. It does happen, but not often.

◆   ◆   ◆

In 1972 while at the Ford-Mercury dealership, one of my salesmen came to me one day insisting I go buy a 1962 Mercury one of our customers was selling. Being busy, I didn't want to take the time, but he persisted. The car, a 1962 Mercury Monterey 2 door hardtop, had less than 3,000 miles on it. He described the owner as a widow lady who literally used the car to go to church on Sunday and the grocery store once a week. The car had never come out or the garage, or been driven in bad or wet weather.

I purchased the car from the woman and gave her the premium asking price for the car. It was in excellent condition for being ten years old. It had one small dent in a side molding, and a hole in the driver's rubber floor mat where she'd pushed her high heel shoe through the mat. This was quite common with the small woman's heels of the sixties.

We had both the body trim piece and the floor mat in parts. We replaced both and detailed the car. We then put the *new* ten-year-old car with only 3,000 miles on the showroom floor. We had a lot of fun watching customer's expressions when we told them about the little old lady who only drove it to the grocery store once a week and to church on Sunday, a totally true story.

We sold the car quickly with no warranty. I explained why there was no warranty to the buyer. This car had probably never been driven over thirty-five miles per hour in ten years. It had never been run long enough to get the engine hot. I explained how to break in the engine gradually. I warned the new owner that if they took the car out at highway speeds right away, the higher engine revolutions and engine heat could damage the piston rings. The customer broke in the engine as advised and got many years of pleasure from the car.

◆　◆　◆

Once, during my days at the recreational vehicle manufacturer, I made a stop at one of our large dealers. He and much of his staff were on a lunch break, so I joined them.

One of the salesmen asked a technical question about why we made our deluxe pickup campers a certain way. I had no idea at the time. I made up a long, complex, and technical explanation. When I got done, there was a long pause before someone asked, "Is that right?" I said "No, but it sure sounded good, didn't it." Everyone had a good laugh.

I offered to get a real answer, but they told me not to bother. Have fun, but never lie to a customer.

◆　◆　◆

I previously mentioned showing value for a tune-up by writing out everything included in a tune-up. Showing value is important, but we still had service customers who were dissatisfied for various reasons.

One of the biggest problems was delivering the customer's car dirty. A greasy steering wheel can be a real turn-off. I quickly changed procedure in the shop to make sure we didn't leave grease on the car.

Most body shops at the time didn't even wash a car before giving it back to the customer. Can you imagine how critical a customer would be if he or she picked up the car with a new fender and bumper, and the rest of the car looked dirty? We washed every car that came out of the body shop.

Today, some service facilities wash and vacuum every car they service. This may not have anything to do with the actual service performed, but makes for a happier customer. Do you pay for this extra service? Of course you do. It's built into the price, but the customer perceives greater value.

Sometimes we still had an unhappy customer. Maybe a misunderstanding, or poor communication, or sometimes my technician didn't complete the job properly. Nobody is perfect.

My service manager was very uncomfortable dealing with customer complaints, and initially called me for every complaint. The first, step is to listen attentively to the complaint. Next, apologize for any inconvenience. The easiest solution at that point is to just ask the customer what they wanted. They hardly ever asked for anything unreasonable. If the request was reasonable, we complied immediately with no haggling.

Sometimes the customer would say, "I don't want anything. I just wanted to bring it to your attention." In this situation, we still offered some discount on the service, or some future service. We also always offered our apology for the second time and thanked the customer for bringing the problem to our attention. After my service manager saw how easy it was to handle customer complaints with this system, he no longer needed me to be involved.

◆ ◆ ◆

We've all heard the saying, "The customer is always right." This is a pretty good guideline for good customer service. Sometimes the customer just wants to be right. Forget the facts. Forget logic. The customer just needs to be right sometimes.

Think about your personal relationship with your spouse or significant other. Sometimes they just have to be right or win. Forget the facts or logic. They just have to win.

I have some great examples, but in the best interests of my happy home, I'll drop it here. Just think about it. You'll get my point.

Your customers are no different. Sometimes they need to be heard. Don't make them wrong. They may not ask for much and you can gain a good customer for the future.

I'm not telling you to give the customer anything

they want. There are some customers who are simply unreasonable. They are few and far between, but they exist. Once, at the car dealership, I arrived one morning and was confronted with a very irate customer. I don't even remember his problem.

He stood by the service counter with a tire iron in his hand threatening me. I found out later that he had previously been convicted of assault. I should have been scared, but for some reason he struck me as funny and I laughed at him. This unnerved him and we started to talk. He became a good customer.

I don't mean to imply that every customer can be saved. There are customers who aren't worth the trouble. These are rare. They'll normally have the reputation as complainers so when they bad-mouth you, no one will take them seriously.

When in the Sparks Computerized Car Care business, I had a new customer come in with a car that requiring a lot of work. After a free inspection, we gave him a list of what the car needed and what the repairs would cost. He said he couldn't afford all the repairs and asked if I would do just a small part of the repairs at this time.

I explained that doing this small part of the repairs wouldn't fix the car, but made the huge mistake of agreeing to do part of the repairs. The business was new and I was hungry for business. I should have insisted on repairing the car correctly or not doing any work on the car.

A new business will often attract problem customers, because existing businesses will no longer do business with them. Be prepared. We did the repairs requested. The car still didn't run properly as all the needed repairs hadn't been performed.

The customer came back complaining that the car didn't run properly. Of course it didn't run properly, we'd only done part of the needed repairs. The customer ignored that fact, and kept saying he'd paid us to repair his car and it still didn't run right. I should never have touched the car.

The customer wouldn't listen to reason and wanted us to repair his car at no additional charge. Since repairing the car correctly would cost several times what he'd previously paid, I asked if he'd like all his money back. He agreed. I said I would write him a check right then with one condition. He would leave and never came back. I thought this probably wasn't good customer management at the time, but several customers in the waiting room had overheard the discussion and started to applaud.

Not all customers are worth the trouble, but try your best. Don't lose any customers who can be saved.

◆　◆　◆

Politics and business do not mix well. Your customer may not feel the same way you feel.

You obviously believe in a capitalist society to some extent or you wouldn't be thinking of going into business. I'm a strong believer in a capitalist society as long as the business adds value. I'm opposed to paper profits that add no value. I think these profits are sometimes immoral, and should even be illegal. This is why we had the banking and economic problems in 2008 and beyond.

You may need to be active in politics for the good

of your business, but be very careful talking politics with your customers. If they don't agree with your political views, you could lose their business.

◆ ◆ ◆

I've seen people in business lose a customer over $100 when the cost of getting a new customer might be three or four times that amount.

Remember when we discussed word of mouth advertising. The same principle works in reverse. An unhappy customer will tell at least ten people. It doesn't take many unhappy customers to give your business a bad reputation. It can mean the difference between profit and loss.

We mentioned the saying "Time is money." It's true in customer service too. Resolve the complaint immediately, so you don't have to waste time on the problem later. You must also respect your customer's time.

Talk to the customer immediately. Delaying the problem only makes it worse. Give the customer what they want, if it's not unreasonable, and do it without delay. It is easier and cheaper to retain a customer than to get a new one.

◆ ◆ ◆

Does good customer service pay? Let me give you an example where it did. There was a large Farm Service Cooperative in the town where I had the Ford-Mercury dealership. They had a good-sized fleet of trucks and pickups.

When I came to town, the Farm Service ran only Chevrolet and GMC vehicles. Five years later, they'd switched almost totally to Ford vehicles.

I took the time and made an effort to find out what they needed for equipment, and made every effort to give them trucks properly equipped to do the job. The price was fair, but the important thing is that the trucks were equipped right for the job. As a consequence, the total cost of operation went down.

I didn't claim the Ford trucks would never break down, but I did promise to get them up and running as fast as possible during a busy season. I knew it was critical to keep equipment moving in seasons such as spring planting. A truck can't move product or make money if it's broken down.

I told the Farm Service manager we would keep our repair shop open around the clock if necessary to keep his trucks moving in the busy seasons. I did say we'd have to charge time and a half for this extra service. He had to make that call.

We didn't work many nights on the Farm Service trucks, but they greatly appreciated it when we did. The over-time labor charge was a minor cost compared to the cost of having a truck out of service.

One day, I was in my office at the dealership with a couple buying a new car. We were haggling over the last $50 to complete the deal. The Farm Service manager stuck his head in the door and said:

Excuse me. I need three F-250 four-wheel drive pickups to pull fertilizer trailers. I need one F-250 two-wheel drive pickup with air conditioning for my Garrison plant manager. I need one F-600 truck for a petroleum delivery

> tank wagon. You know how to spec them.
> Order them. Thanks. Sorry for interrupting.

The trust the manager showed came from good customer service. Impressed by this, the couple in my office finished their new car purchase. Good customer service does produce satisfied customers and additional sales.

◆　◆　◆

Customer service is pretty simple. Treat the customer, as you'd like to be treated. Communicate with the customer in a timely manner and never ever lie to the customer.

Honesty is a good rule in all aspects of business. We should be just as honest in our business life as in our personal life.

I once was the president of a church when we were without a minister. One Sunday, we couldn't arrange for a visiting minister to preach the sermon, and as president of the congregation, I got drafted for the job. I talked about how some people had different levels of morality in church, at home, and at work. There should be no difference.

As a kid, I remember asking my dad why someone in our small community had been nicknamed Windy. Dad replied, "Because you can't believe or trust anything he says." In our small community people knew whom they could trust and whose word was good.

A person's word meant everything to my dad. He was a tenant farmer on the farm where he raised me for sixteen years from age two. He only had a written lease for the first year. The next fifteen years were done on a handshake. Maybe it was a better time.

As we do business today in a national or even an international market, it's not as easy to know whose word is good. Will honesty in business reward you financially? Maybe and maybe not, but hopefully you'll feel better about yourself if your word is good.

We all know of people who have benefited, at least in the short run, by being dishonest. Often this benefit is short lived. I personally know of an individual who's been disowned by his family because he lied to, and cheated members of his own family. He paid a big price in my opinion.

Success in business is much easier if you're honest and make your word your bond. You'll probably sleep better at night too. Jon Huntsman Sr. is a good example. His word is his bond and sometimes may have cost him money in the short run, but today Jon is a billionaire who's done many good things with his success including the Huntsman Cancer Foundation.

◆ ◆ ◆

There are many examples of people who are honest in business and very successful. Paul J. Meyers is another example that comes to mind. I met Paul in the collector car business. He likes 1936 Fords and has an outstanding collection.

John Edmund Haggai wrote Paul's biography called *Paul J. Meyer and the Art of Giving*. At the time the book was written in 1994, Paul gave $342,000 per month to charity and his net worth was going up. That's what I call successful, and Paul is probably honest to a fault.

Paul is very successful in many ways including financially. He started writing at the age of seventy. Paul sent me an autographed copy of his first book *I Inherited a Fortune.* Paul never inherited a dime, but he learned how to work, and he made his word his bond.

Chapter 19: Distribution Systems

Almost every business distributes some sort of product or service. A product doesn't have to be tangible. An insurance policy is a product, but not tangible except for the paper. Every business needs inventory, equipment, materials, and supplies.

How does a business obtain the needed inventory, equipment, materials, and supplies? How does a business get the products or services sold to the consumer?

We should take a quick look at the various distribution systems. The first distinction is retail versus wholesale. A retail business means the business is selling a product or service to the end user. A Wal-Mart store is considered retail as most customers are buying products for their personal or family use.

A Sam's Club store will be both retail and wholesale. Some customers will be buying for their personal and family use. Businesses will also use Sam's Club. These businesses will consume some of the products purchased at Sam's Club, and these purchases are considered retail as the product is consumed by the business. Businesses may also purchase products at Sam's Club that they will resell to their customers, and these are considered a wholesale transaction.

Some businesses are only wholesalers. They don't sell to the general public, or to the end consumer.

In the Ford-Mercury dealership, I used automobile auctions that were only for licensed dealers. These auctions didn't allow the public to attend or buy at the auction. Cars bought and sold at a *Dealer Only* auction would be considered a wholesale transaction.

When in the collector car business, I used auctions that were open to the public. Dealers were buying cars for resale, making them wholesale buyers. The collectors buying cars for their private collections were retail buyers.

◆　◆　◆

Some businesses are exclusively retail and some are exclusively wholesale, others are both. At the Ford-Mercury dealership, we had many departments. We had new cars that we sold to the public at retail, but we also did dealer trades and wholesaled new cars to other Ford and Mercury dealers.

We took in used cars on trade. I retailed about half those trade-ins, and wholesaled the other half at *Dealer Only* auctions. I also occasionally bought used cars at auction, which would be a wholesale purchase.

The dealership also had a service department and a body shop that were totally retail operations except for internal sales on owned inventory which would be considered wholesale sales. We had a parts department that was both retail and wholesale. The parts department supplied parts to our service department and body shop. Parts department counter sales included parts sold to the public at retail and wholesale parts sales to other automobile repair businesses.

We also had a finance and insurance department, a leasing department, and a daily rental department. All of these were retail operations.

Ford evaluated every dealership based on what they called P*lanning Volume*. This started with the number of new cars they expected a particular dealership to sell each year. They then expected the dealer to make some average gross on the new vehicle sales with a specified variance in individual grosses.

Used car retail sales were expected to be some percentage of new car sales with some average gross and some specified range of grosses. Cars wholesaled were not considered a profit center, but weren't expected to lose money. The thinking was that trade-in values should be realistic wholesale values if we were going to be competitive in the market. I usually made a decision to retail or wholesale every trade-in at the time I appraised it. It's impossible to correctly appraise every trade-in, but the last three years at the dealership we made an average profit of $5 per unit for every used car wholesaled. This indicated good appraising.

Every other department was expected to do a specific dollar volume and profit based on the *Planning Volume*. For example, the parts department was expected to do so much volume with the service department, so much with the body shop, so much in retail counter sales, and so much volume wholesale counter sales.

Ford wanted a dealership to meet *Planning Volume* guides in all departments and areas. They wanted warranty claims to be a given percentage of new car sales. Ford also wanted good customer relations with a low number of customer complaints. Ford used a report card system that every customer could send to Ford.

If a dealership met all these requirements, it could receive Ford's Total Excellence in Customer Service award. Very few dealerships ever received this award. We consistently performed at 145% of our planning guide and did receive the Total Excellence in Customer Service award.

◆　◆　◆

Manufacturing companies often only wholesale their products. They may do little or no retail sales. Manufacturing companies are often referred to as OEM or Original Equipment Manufacturer.

You may hear people say, "I bought it direct from the manufacturer or OEM, so I got a really good deal." The idea is that by buying direct from the OEM, they've cut out all middlemen and their markups. This is true in some cases, but not all.

Many manufacturers will not sell direct to the retail buyer. Those that do may charge retail prices.

The RV manufacturing plant I ran was located in a small town where I didn't have a retail dealer. We didn't promote retail sales from the plant, but since we didn't have a retail dealer in the town, people would come to the plant to buy direct.

We would sell direct to the retail buyer that came to the plant, but we always charged what we considered the manufacturer's suggested retail price. We didn't discount the product. The retail buyer that came to our plant didn't save by buying direct from the manufacturer. In fact, he probably could have bought it cheaper from any of our dealers, as most discounted our products. We didn't discount any sales made directly from the plant, because I didn't want any of our dealers to get the idea that we were in competition with them.

◆ ◆ ◆

One type of business that doesn't deal with the public and could be either retail or wholesale is called *Business to Business*, and is often referred to as "B2B". *Business to Business* means a business that only sells or provides a service to other businesses and not retail customers.

If the business buying the goods or services is consuming the goods or services it's a retail purchase. The purchase is a wholesale purchase if they are reselling to the end user. One nice feature of *Business to Business* is that the hours of operation are normally closer to a traditional workweek and not the hours required by most retail businesses.

◆ ◆ ◆

Sales and marketing is a big part of the distribution system. Sales clerks, sales representatives, and sales agents perform sales activities. Many other names will be used with today's love of buzz words, but most sales people will fall into one of these three categories.

The sales clerk is the first and has probably the least responsibility. Sales clerks usually work at a retail store. They assist the customer and have very little authority to negotiate price, set terms, or determine any conditions of the sale. Sales clerks are almost always employees. They may be salaried or hourly. They may or may not receive commission in addition to their base pay.

Sales representatives or sales reps usually have more responsibility than a sales clerk. Sales reps may work at a retail facility or they may go to the customer. Sales reps usually work on salary plus commission, or straight commission. If the sales rep is working on straight commission, he or she may be an independent contractor. The sales rep has little or no authority to make or negotiate price, terms or conditions of the sales.

The sales agent is a legal agent for the company, and does have legal authority to negotiate terms and conditions of the sale on behalf of the company he or she represents. They may work on straight salary, or salary plus commission, or straight commission with a guarantee. A bonus may be in addition to any of the above.

The sales agent is usually an employee of the company since he or she can negotiate for the company. There are exceptions such as insurance agents. Legally, some insurance agents are considered independent in spite of the fact that in most cases they are legal agents for the insurance companies they represent.

◆　◆　◆

Let's take a look at the physical distribution of products. A product makes its way to the end user. The product is produced by the original equipment manufacturer.

The product may then be stored in a warehouse, owned by the manufacturer, a wholesaler, or a third party. The warehouse owner may or may not take ownership of the product. If the warehouse owner takes ownership of the product, the warehouse owner is then acting as a wholesaler or retailer, and is responsible for marketing the product. The product may then be shipped to a retailer. The retailer sells and delivers the product to the end consumer.

There are many variations of this process. The manufacturer may sell to one wholesaler or a number of wholesalers. The manufacturer may sell direct to the retailer. A variety of sales personnel previously discussed may be used.

The manufacturer may sell direct to the consumer. This is referred to as *buying direct* or *buying OEM*. This may be done through a variety of marketing methods including catalogs and the Internet.

◆　◆　◆

Wholesalers may sell to retailers and/or end users. The wholesaler will use the same marketing methods used by the manufacturer. A wholesaler may or may not take physical possession of the product.

Retailers sell and deliver the product or service to the consumer, or end user. The consumer may come to the retail store, and the product may be picked up by the consumer or delivered to the consumer. The retailer may go directly to the consumer to make the sale and delivery.

There are many variations of how a retail sale and delivery are completed. For example, the Internet has many sites marketing products to many consumers. The person owning the web site in many cases will never take physical possession of the product. They will not have ownership of the product until after they have sold the product.

All the same distribution channels apply when the product is a service or an intangible except for the physical warehousing function.

♦ ♦ ♦

We talked about shipping costs in the chapter on pricing. Remember, freight charges don't add value in the consumers mind. A higher price is more likely to add perceived value.

The KISS principle really is applicable when considering shipping, packaging, and handling. KISS stands for "Keep It Simple Stupid." Use a standardized shipping and handling charge if possible. Building the cost of shipping into the price and having free shipping is even better. Customers like *free* shipping.

If you're selling on the Internet, the customer must be able to see what their total cost is without having to take the initiative to call, or initiate placing an order. This is just an extra step they may not make in some cases. They will go to a competitor. They do not care if your end cost may be better in the end. Remember to "Keep It Simple Stupid."

♦ ♦ ♦

As you investigate any business, make sure you totally understand the supply side and the distribution process for the product or service you're offering, and understand your role in the process.

You must be comfortable that you can rely on the supply and distribution side of your business. You can't make sales and profit if you can't supply the product or service.

In the collector car business, sales came easily. The supply side was the hard part of the business. I couldn't just call the factory and order a new 1965 Pontiac GTO convertible. I had to find and maybe restore that vehicle before I could sell it, and I still had to get it at a price where I could make a profit.

Chapter 20: Financing

Financing is a major part of starting any business. As I've previously stated, under capitalization is the number one cause of new business failure in my opinion.

When a business is undercapitalized, there is eventually a cash flow problem. When this occurs it's normal to start cutting expenses. Some of the first things to go are things like housekeeping and staff like receptionists. We've all walked into dirty businesses where no one greeted us. We might think the business is in trouble, and we seldom do business with that company.

Another area cuts are made is in marketing. Some accountants consider marketing activities such as advertising as an expense that can be cut. That step is often a death sentence for the business.

Also, don't make the mistake of thinking you'll grow and generate cash flow. Often, growth eats up capital instead of generating cash. Remember the example I gave of tripling sales in ninety days when I started Lee Motors, Inc.

◆ ◆ ◆

The Wednesday, October 18, 2006 issue of *USA TODAY* had an interesting article titled "Where do start-ups get their money?" They quoted banking giant Wells Fargo who'd found in a recent survey of owners that their start-up costs averaged just $10,000.

USA TODAY listed the following sources for financing start-ups according to the Small Business Administration.

- 57%   Personal/family savings
- 12%   Bank business loan
- 9%   Personal/business credit cards
- 9%   Personal/family assets such as second mortgages
- 3%   Outside investors including venture capital
- 1%   Government guaranteed bank loan
- 1%   Business loan from government

I have some opinions on these figures. With an average investment of $10,000, the survey obviously includes a lot of small independent start-ups. We'll talk about these. There are some huge success stories for independent start-up businesses, but most just create a job for the owner, or fail.

Having adequate personal savings available to fund a business is obviously the ideal situation. This is possible if the total investment needed is relatively small, but most businesses require an investment that's more than most people have available in cash.

♦ ♦ ♦

In chapter three, "Myths About Starting a Business," we have already addressed how banks do not make business loans. Banks certainly do not make loans based on a business plan.

I once heard a banker say that they were not investors, but provided financial assistance based on equity in hard assets. Equity in hard assets is really what determines the loan a bank will make. They may loan up to 80% of an asset's value less any encumbrances. They may loan as low as 40% of the value of an asset less any encumbrances depending on the type of asset.

One time when I opened an automobile service franchise with silent partners, the bank wanted personal assets pledged that totaled over 300% of the loan amount. It made more sense to liquidate some of the assets and cash fund the project. This is what we did.

Banks want the principal responsible for running the business to have prior experience in the industry in which they are starting a business. If the owner does not have experience in the industry, the bank will want to know someone that does have experience in that industry is involved in the management of the business. The exception is when the loan is for a franchise. Most banks understand that a franchise provides a proven business system, training, and support so prior experience in the industry is not needed.

In addition to pledged assets, banks look at your credit rating. This is more and more important in today's banking environment. However, you have to owe money and be making payments to have a really good credit rating. Someone who doesn't have any debt and isn't making monthly payments won't have as good a credit score as someone with debt. Sound stupid? Yes, but that's the way it works. Nobody ever said things have to make sense.

There was a time when banks looked at the individual's character, but this is a thing of the past. Banks today are bigger and less personal. With the exception of small independent, community banks, a banker doesn't know their customers personally. The banker from a big bank doesn't know anything about their customer's character in most cases.

◆　◆　◆

At nineteen, I considered starting farming. I was married with one child and had an opportunity to rent 400 acres. My dad planned to retire from farming in three years. I thought we could farm together for those three years, and I would buy out his equipment over that three-year period.

I needed to borrow enough money to buy a bigger tractor, bigger plow, bigger disc, and a flatbed to move equipment. I hated milking, but I needed to buy some milk cows to provide regular income for the first few years. I needed to borrow $10,000 to buy the equipment and milk cows. $10,000 then is probably equivalent to $70,000 or $80,000 today.

As a nineteen-year-old kid, I went to see Wilford Rood at Bode State Bank. I told him I needed to borrow $10,000. He said "Okay." I asked him if he wanted to know why I wanted the money. He said, "No, I know who you are." Maybe local, independent banks did things right then.

Unfortunately, banks don't make loans based on

character any more. I think they were better off when they knew their customers, and did make loans on character. Unfortunately, that practice is just history now. Bank examiners wouldn't allow a bank to make a loan based on the customer's character. Today, you need a good credit score and collateral.

◆ ◆ ◆

Home equity is the most frequently used asset to fund a business requiring an investment too large to fund with cash and other liquid assets. For businesses that require a larger investment, a home equity loan or refinancing your home is a good option.

A home equity loan or refinancing is easier to obtain than a *business loan* using the home as collateral. The interest rate will probably be lower than the rate on a business loan. Don't ask me why. That's just the way it is.

Obviously, if you're quitting your job to start the business, refinance or obtain the home equity loan before you quit your job. Mortgage companies prefer people with a job history and not a new business.

◆ ◆ ◆

I attended an entrepreneur's club meeting when a woman commented that she didn't want to take out a home equity loan to start her business because she didn't want to put her home at risk.

We tried to explain that with a home equity loan the risk would be limited to the home. With a business loan, the bank would want her to guarantee the loan personally which would put all her assets at risk including her home.

When putting up assets as collateral for a loan,

always pledge specific assets if possible. This limits your financial exposure to those pledged assets. Remember that just *personally securing* a loan puts all your assets at risk.

The woman mentioned above was under the false impression that the bank would be assuming the risk with a business loan and she wouldn't have any risk. Remember, banks are not venture capitalists or partners. Banks don't make business loans based on a business plan.

◆ ◆ ◆

The Small Business Administration (SBA) guarantees some business loans. A bank or some other financial institution makes the loan. The SBA then guarantees some percentage of the loan so the bank's liability is limited.

Don't think this limits your liability for the loan. You'll still be personally liable in most cases. You'll still need to secure the loan with hard assets. Nothing has changed in this respect. You'll probably pay a little higher interest rate with an SBA guaranteed loan. The biggest advantage is that the bank may make the loan when they wouldn't without the SBA guarantee.

Applying for an SBA guaranteed loan is a good exercise. It will make you do your homework. I've applied for several SBA loans, but I've never had one. By the time I qualified for the SBA guaranteed loan, I could get the money with better terms without the SBA guarantee.

There's one exception in my opinion. Some franchises are pre-approved for SBA loans. They may even have designated lenders ready to make the loans.

I know of one case where a lender was willing to loan 85% of the total initial investment. This is exceptional and very rare. Normally, a loan isn't for that high a percentage of the initial investment.

For a business without hard assets included in the initial investment, a maximum loan will only be 50%, or less, of the initial start-up cost for businesses. The bank will still want the loan 100% secured with pledged assets.

◆ ◆ ◆

There are occasionally some government loans and grants available. Grants are usually for relatively small amounts and very limited in number. The Small Business Administration does make a few direct loans.

Government grants and SBA direct loans are usually reserved for women or racial minorities. I once told an SBA administrator I was Norwegian and that was a minority. The SBA administrator just laughed.

I've had clients say they were going to put their business in their wife's name because of all the money available for a woman starting businesses. Not true.

I spoke at a "How to Start a Business" class when the other guest speaker was a woman working with an economic development organization. A major part of her job was to find funding for new and expanding businesses. She mentioned how many people had the false impression of money available for women starting business. She said "If that were true, I would have my own business and not be working in this job."

◆ ◆ ◆

Your 401K or other retirement account could provide all or part of the funding needed for your

173

business venture. You can take an early withdrawal of your money, but you'll pay a penalty and income tax on the money. This option is pretty unattractive in most cases.

Many retirement accounts allow you to borrow from your account. The interest rate and terms are usually reasonable.

The law also allows you to invest the money from your retirement account in your own corporation. At this time, I believe the corporation must be a "C" corporation, and not an "S" corporation or a Limited Liability Corporation for this financing option.

You'll need to find an attorney or firm familiar with this financing option. There are several firms now specializing in this service. There will be an initial cost and an annual fee, but it will probably be less than you'd pay in interest for some other financing options.

◆ ◆ ◆

Another potential source of funding is life insurance policies. There are two types of life insurance: They are *Permanent* and *Term*. Term insurance gives protection for some period of time, but doesn't build any cash value. Permanent policies can be whole life, universal life, limited pay, or endowments. All permanent policies may have some cash value.

The *Cash Value* is the amount you'll receive if you cancel the policy. Remember, you'll probably have to pay tax on the money.

A better option is to borrow from the cash value. The interest rate is usually low and the payment terms flexible.

Credit cards may be a source of short-term funding. The interest rates can be very attractive. I've seen 0% interest on cash advances on credit cards for up to a year.

Be very careful of this funding source. Interest rates can jump to over 20%. You must be confident you'll be able to make the payments and pay off the account before the interest rate increases.

♦ ♦ ♦

I should talk about *Float*. Shortly after I sold Lee Motors, Inc., I went on a trip with the Chairman of the Board for the company employing me. He mentioned float. I asked him what he meant. He started to explain, but suddenly stopped when he remembered I'd been a car dealer. He said "You SOB. You were a car dealer. You guys invented float."

There was some truth in his statement. I've previously talked about floorplan financing for new vehicle inventory. As soon as the dealer sells a vehicle, he pays the finance source for that vehicle.

If the dealer is short on operating capital, it is very tempting to use the money from the sold vehicle for operating expenses and delay paying off the vehicle on floorplan. This can be a short-term solution to a cash flow problem, but it is only a short-term solution.

The dealer hopes cash flow will improve and take care of the problem. Maybe he has a large used vehicle inventory that he owns and can wholesale to generate the cash needed.

A dealer that is floating inventory is normally referred to as being *Out of Trust*. This is a sign that the dealership is in trouble and they will probably lose the franchise and the business will be sold or closed if more capital is not pumped into the business.

Denny Hecker was considered the largest and most successful automobile dealer in Minnesota. When his businesses went bad, he started shifting money from one business to another. He used float extensively.

When Chrysler Financial caught Hecker *Out of Trust*, his whole world collapsed. He had personally secured most of his loans. He had no choice but to declare bankruptcy. He was later convicted of fraud and sentenced to jail.

There are all kinds of financial floats. Most can be called fraud. I definitely do not recommend using float as a finance source.

◆　◆　◆

Venture capitalist companies are a possibility if you have a business with the potential to generate huge profits. A venture capitalist is willing to take a risk if the potential return is great enough. One venture capitalist told me that only one out of ten ventures they fund make it, but that one will generate huge profits.

Venture capital companies usually look for an established company that's had some breakthrough that needs a capital infusion to implement and grow. Venture capital companies usually specialize in a specific area or industry where they have expertise, such as new medical technology.

Venture capital companies will provide capital and share in the risk, but they'll have conditions. They may also provide expertise in various areas of the business.

They'll probably want some management control. You'll give up some control of your company. You will definitely give up a large portion of the profits.

◆　◆　◆

Family and friends are common sources of funding for buying or starting a business. Next to savings and home equity, this is the most common source of funding. Most people say they would never consider getting money from family or friends, but many do when it gets down to crunch time.

I worked with one couple that said family wasn't an option for financing. Later, when he told his father what they were trying to do, the father made them an offer.

The father owned a condo free and clear. The father offered to take out a mortgage on the condo and give the money to the son for the business. The son would then make the mortgage payments.

This arrangement provided the son with a long-term loan for the business at a rate and payment they never could have obtained with a business loan. I assume the son signed some kind of note with his father, but maybe not.

Loans from friends and relatives are a viable option for financing a business. A loan is not a partnership.

Chapter 21: Partnerships

Partnerships are such an important decision for anyone going into business that I decided to devote an entire chapter to the topic.

Don't even think about a Partnership!

Partnerships do not work!

Partnerships are nothing but trouble!

There are no exceptions!

Partnerships do not work!

◆   ◆   ◆

Now let me tell you how I really feel about partnerships. They don't work.

People often think of partnerships as a means of financing. Don't. Don't even think about it. Don't even think about a partnership. True partnerships don't work. I will repeat. Partnerships don't work.

I know an individual who works in franchise development that previously owned a large and successful franchise. He bought the franchise with a partner. He claims the partnership worked out well only because he bought his partner out before they ever started operations. He will not recommend awarding a franchise to any partnership.

I also refuse to work with any partnership. I'm defining a partnership as two or more individuals investing in and working in a business. This is sometimes referred to as a *General Partnership*. A limited partnership, silent investors, and loans don't meet my definition of a partnership. We'll talk more about them later.

◆ ◆ ◆

I've seen best friends go into business together. They both had talents that complimented each other. They'd worked together in their jobs. They loved working together. This has to be an exception, right? Wrong.

If the business has problems, and most do have hard times, each will blame the other. Even if the business is great from day one and the two guys remain best friends, this will not hold true for their wives. There will be trouble.

Eventually, one partner will have to buy the other

out or the business will fail. If the problem cannot be resolved between the partners, it'll eventually have to be sold at a loss.

I can think of a restaurant, a resort, and a planned area development for a golf course and condominiums that have all been bought or started as partnerships in the lake area where I live in the last few years.

All three business ventures have failed at least partly because they were partnerships. The really sad thing is that several families have had to take out personal bankruptcy as a result.

◆　◆　◆

I have a distant relative that we'll call Tom. Tom went into business with one of his best friends. Both individuals had their own businesses. The partnership was strictly an investment. Luckily, they set the business up as a corporation and not a general partnership. Neither partner worked actively in the business on a full-time basis.

The business seemed to do well, but never made any money. Eventually, an audit revealed Tom's partner had been skimming the business. He'd have the business pay some of his personal bills and expenses. For example, he had the business pay property taxes on his personal real estate.

By the time the audit ended, they discovered over one million dollars had been embezzled. Tom could have had his ex-friend sent to prison, but that wouldn't have gotten the money back.

Luckily, Tom could afford the loss and took sole ownership of the business. Even best friends don't seem to work out.

Close relatives should be an exception, right? Wrong. I have a friend that we'll call Jane. Jane has one brother. Their parents owned a very successful independent business, which they inherited.

Neither Jane nor her brother was active in the business. The business had good management, and had made good money in the past. Then things started to change. Sales started to decline due to increased competition from franchise competitors. As an independent, they could also not buy as well as some of their franchise competition. Profits declined.

The business continually needed more operating capital. Jane and her brother continued to borrow money to keep the business going. The bank requested and received personal guarantees for these loans.

Eventually, the business went bankrupt. Jane then discovered that her brother had been skimming, or embezzling, from the business for years. Since the business was a true partnership, all notes had been signed personally. The lenders would go after whoever had money. Since Jane's brother had no money, the lenders went after Jane and her husband. It wiped out their savings to pay off the business loans.

My friend not only lost the business and their savings, it hurt her family. Partnerships don't work.

♦ ♦ ♦

I had a client tell me their potential partner was their best friend, and they'd known each other their entire life so it would work. If you become partners with your best friend, you'll no longer be best friends. I guarantee you will not agree on everything in business and consequently will not remain best friends. Even if you and your partner do agree on everything, your spouses won't, and eventually the spouses will break up the partnership.

One exception I've seen that worked was a partnership of three brothers. Their father had started the business. All three brothers worked in the business. The father set the job descriptions and responsibilities for each brother.

After the father's retirement, the three brothers continued in their previously defined positions. The partnership worked successfully for many years.

♦ ♦ ♦

I know of another example where two brothers took over their father's car dealership. One brother ran the new and used car departments. The other brother ran the parts and service departments. They both had the same responsibility as when their father owned the dealership. They stayed out of each other's way, the wives stayed out of the business, and they ran a very successful automobile dealership for many years.

The two brothers eventually had to dissolve the partnership when their children got old enough to work in the business. It no longer worked. They bought a second dealership and each brother took their own dealership.

♦ ♦ ♦

I once had two individuals referred to me who were going to be laid off. They were victims of a merger and the new company planned on shutting down the operation where they worked. They planned on going into business as partners, because they'd worked well together for years.

I told them my opinion on partnerships. I recommended they talk and be clear about what both expected the relationship to be in the partnership.

The woman had been the man's boss. She assumed the relationship would remain the same, with her in the position of authority. The man expected to be an equal in the new relationship. After talking, they decided to go their separate ways. They avoided a very costly mistake with a partnership.

◆ ◆ ◆

There are very few exceptions. Obviously, a marriage is a partnership and can be a business partnership too. We all know how many marriages end in divorce.

I had a married couple as clients who found a business model that fit their goals and needs. The business succeeded, grew, and expanded until the divorce. The business then had to be sold, and sold quickly at a loss. I believe divorce is the number one cause of failure for clients I've worked with personally.

◆ ◆ ◆

Limited partnerships can be another way of funding for starting or buying a business. Limited partnerships are quite common in real estate. The important distinction between a limited partnership and a general partnership is that with a limited partnership the limited control of the limited partners is distinctly spelled out in the agreement, and only the general partner is active in the business. If this option sounds interesting to you, find an attorney familiar with limited partnerships in your state. Be sure you understand your obligations and liabilities.

◆　◆　◆

The best opportunity created by partnerships is for the individual who comes in after the partnership has failed and the business is sold at a loss. It may be a bank foreclosure sale, a bankruptcy liquidation sale, or just a quick sale to get out of the partnership.

Failed partnerships can be very good buys for a new investor. The downside is that the business is almost guaranteed to be run down and will have to be built back up to be profitable.

Chapter 22: Legal Structure

What should be the legal structure of your business? You can be a Sole Proprietor, a Partnership, a Limited Liability Corporation, an "S" Corporation, or a "C" corporation. There is no ideal answer that fits all situations.

I'll try to give a brief and oversimplified explanation of each. A *Sole Proprietor* is just that. You own it. The profits are yours and the liabilities are yours. Income is yours personally for tax purposes.

We've already talked about partnerships. Forget about any true general partnerships. Liability in a general partnership is also interesting. You might think you have only 50% of the liability if you're in a 50-50 partnership. Wrong, any liability could be 100% yours. A creditor will go after anyone who has money. If you have more liquid assets than your partner, they will come after you and forget your partner.

A *Limited Liability* corporation is basically a way to limit personal liability. Don't get the idea that you can eliminate all liability by incorporating. This legal loophole, AKA the *Corporate Veil*, is being closed. We now see officers of corporations not only liable, but serving prison time.

An "S" corporation is a corporation where profits are taken personally based on the percentage of stock ownership. If you own 25% of an "S" Corporation, you will pay personal taxes on 25% of the profits.

♦ ♦ ♦

A "C" corporation is the traditional corporation paying corporate taxes. This option limits your liability the most, unless you personally secure loans to the corporation.

You may or may not draw a salary in any legal structure. Obviously, you have to have something for living expenses. You can live off savings or draw a salary.

Many people are under the impression that they can limit their financial exposure by incorporating. This is true to some extent, but a financial institution will probably want you to personally guarantee any loans unless the corporation is already very well funded with substantial assets.

Most banks look for all the assets they can get to secure a loan. They will not make a loan to a corporation without substantial assets. They'll ask you to pledge personal assets or personally guarantee the loan if the corporation doesn't have adequate assets for collateral. As we discussed in the financing section, personally securing a loan puts you at the most personal risk.

♦ ♦ ♦

If you are a corporation with common stock, you will probably not be a publicly traded corporation. Your corporation will be privately held, at least initially.

How many stockholders will there be? There may be state and federal regulations on how many stockholders you can have before you become subject to state and federal securities laws.

Will the corporation be closed or open? With a closed corporation, the sale of stock may be controlled with the by-laws of the corporation. With an open corporation, a stockholder can sell their stock to anyone.

There are many considerations in determining the best legal structure for your business. There is no right answer for everyone.

How you finance your business may determine the most desirable legal structure of your business. You must make your own choice with the help of your accountant and attorney. Find the right choice for your personal situation.

Chapter 23: Insurance & Government Regulations

When we think about starting a business, we think about how the government might help us with grants and loans. We often don't think about how they might hamper our business and cost us money.

This can be a major consideration for any business decision. Be aware of all government laws, licenses, and regulations that might affect your business.

◆ ◆ ◆

My first insurance class at the University of Iowa was called General Insurance. There were three sections of the class that semester, and luckily the head of the university insurance department taught my section. Professor Emmett J. Vaughan not only knew his subject, he could teach. He's the best instructor I ever had in school.

The sole objective of the course was to teach us how to read a family auto policy, a homeowner's policy, a term life policy, and a whole life policy. Sounds like a simple course, right?

I still remember one of his test questions on the final exam in 1965. This is not really relevant, but fun, and will give you some idea of the level of the class. The amounts will seem small, but remember this is 1965.

Rosie lived in a home she owned. Her sister lived with her. Rosie owned a 1948 Nash and had a minimum standard auto policy of $10,000–$20,000–

$5,000 with $500 medical. Rosie's sister wasn't named on the policy.

Rosie walked to work one day and her sister took the Nash without permission. Rosie's sister came upon a driver whose truck had broken down. She knew the truck driver and offered to help. The truck driver pulled a trailer. The trailer held a statue of Venus de Milo and a live horse. The Nash had a trailer hitch, so they hooked the trailer behind the Nash.

Rosie's sister then drove down the city streets at speeds over 90 MPH. The truck driver riding with her laughed and urged her to go faster. Rosie's sister then hit a refrigerated meat truck at an intersection. The meat truck had the right-of-way.

As a result of the accident, the Nash, the meat truck, and the trailer were totaled, the horse died, the statue of Venus de Milo was in a thousand pieces, and the meat in the meat truck spoiled. Rosie's sister, the truck driver riding with her, and the meat truck driver were all seriously injured. Rosie was also seriously injured by a piece of frozen meat that flew out of the meat truck and hit her while she walked down the sidewalk.

Now, what is covered or not covered under each section of the policy, and why or why not? If covered, what amount is the coverage?

The real kicker is Rosie's injury. Since Rosie was neither hit by a vehicle, nor riding in a vehicle, she is not covered under the $500 medical portion of the policy. She does have the option of collecting under the personal injury portion of her policy up to the $10,000 individual personal injury liability limit and the $20,000 total personal injury liability limit.

❖ ❖ ❖

After the General Insurance class Emmett told me I now knew more about insurance than 9 out of 10 people working in the insurance industry. I thought he was kidding at the time. I later learned he was right. I took two additional insurance classes from Emmett.

Emmett went on to become one of the leading names in insurance nationally. He wrote many of our state insurance exams. He is also the author of *Fundamentals of Risk and Insurance*, which is now in its 10th edition.

I considered Emmett a friend. He also became a potential investor in a venture called Automobile Restorers, which never materialized. This is the venture I was working on when I wrote the piece to *Entrepreneur* magazine detailed in the introduction to this book.

Emmett died in 2004. He will be missed.

❖ ❖ ❖

My point is, there are several types of insurance you will need in your business, and you don't have time to learn everything you need to know about insurance, so you need an expert. I would recommend interviewing several agents before selecting one to work with.

The insurance agent that handles your personal insurance now may be a nice person, but may not have the knowledge you'll need for your business. Friendship is great, but this is business.

Every business has special exposures and liabilities. As a car dealer, I needed *Garage Keeper's*

Legal Liability insurance. If you are not in a business dealing with cars, trucks, or motorcycles, you don't need this type of insurance coverage.

I'd recommend some kind of general liability umbrella coverage. Our country has become very litigious and some of the awards run in the millions. This type of coverage is relatively cheap.

Another thing you may not think of is *Key Man* term life coverage. Any individual who is essential to the success of the business should be insured.

There are many other considerations like fire insurance, flood insurance, and business interruption insurance to name a few. Some businesses now even buy insurance to pay kidnap ransoms for employees. What is becoming of our country?

As Emmett Vaughan taught me, you probably can't afford to insure against every possible risk. If you do, the premiums may eat up all your profits. You'll have to assume some of the risk.

◆ ◆ ◆

If you have employees, you may want to offer health insurance. Your state and maybe the federal government may not give you a choice. If you have a choice, you may want to give health insurance to the officers of the corporation, but not other employees. This is one of the few ways you can discriminate with health insurance.

I recommend looking at medical savings plans combined with high deductible major medical plans. I find this option very desirable as compared to expensive *first dollar coverage* medical plans.

◆ ◆ ◆

If you have employees, you'll have unemployment insurance. You'll pay some standard rate based on your type of business if you're a new business. If you are buying an existing business, the rate will already be determined by how many former employees have drawn on the benefit.

Worker's Compensation is a government-required insurance. The classification of your employees will determine the rate you pay. This is an important consideration.

A few years ago, California decided to classify people cleaning homes and offices the same as construction laborers. The cost of this labor classification almost put cleaning companies out of business. Cleaning franchises stopped selling franchises in the state of California until the state changed the labor classification.

State and federal governments sometimes get a little screwy with legislation. Sometimes this is just a mistake with good intentions.

Most government legislation tends to help the big corporations and hurt small business. This makes sense, as big business can afford lobbyists and campaign contributions to protect their interests.

Don't ignore all the possible government regulations that can or will affect your business. Did you know 40,000 new laws went into effect on January 1, 2012? You may have federal, state, county, and city laws, regulations and permits that affect your business. It is up to you to investigate all of these.

You'll have to determine what sales taxes you need to collect with your business. You may need a variety of licenses in your city or state. You may have zoning laws to deal with. The list goes on and on. Isn't our growing government great?

♦   ♦   ♦

When I worked for the RV manufacturing company, we had a plant located in Pennsylvania. That plant sold to several surrounding states, except for one. That state had such ridiculous consumer protection and product liability laws affecting our product that the company decided not to sell in the state. It wasn't worth the liability and trouble to do business in that state.

This made retail recreational vehicle dealers in the state very unhappy. They called our plant in Pennsylvania wanting to handle our product line. We told them we didn't do business in that state and wouldn't be doing business in that state as long as the state had the current consumer protection and product liability laws.

These laws hurt the consumer in the long run. I would hope this state has their act together by now, but who knows. Government does some really dumb things.

Dealing with local bureaucrats can be both interesting and frustrating. Learn to play the game and try to have fun with it.

Once, in a previous life, I was in the construction business. When we would design a large project we always intentionally removed a couple obvious things from the plans before we submitted them to the appropriate planning and zoning department.

For example, we would remove an obviously

required sidewalk along the street from the plans. The zoning commission could then tell us to add the sidewalk. By omitting a couple obvious things like the sidewalk for the planning commission to find, they could justify their job and everyone was happy.

The sidewalk was always on the master plans, but if we submitted the completed, correct plans, the planning commission would have to find something else wrong to justify their job. There's nothing wrong with asking for more than you expect to get. Play the game and don't be confrontational.

It's your responsibility to check with the appropriate government offices for regulations that will affect your business. Your accountant and attorney may be able to help you identify and comply with these regulations.

If you're buying a franchise, your franchisor should be a big help. If you're buying an existing business, check that the business is currently observing all regulations and laws.

◆　◆　◆

Don't make the mistake of thinking your business is so small that it can stay under the government radar. You'll probably get caught no matter how small you are.

President Nixon imposed wage and price controls in 1971 when I was a Ford-Mercury dealer. We complied. A few months later, Ford Motor Company raised the price on parts. Ford raised the price on all parts sold from inventory, newly purchased, or newly manufactured. Ford had the approval of the federal government for this price increase. Lee Motors, Inc.

also raised its price on parts to the new suggested retail price.

Within a few months, the feds came into Lee Motors, Inc. and said we were in violation of the price controls. They said we couldn't raise the price on any parts that we had in inventory. We could only raise the price on parts purchased from Ford after Ford had raised the price.

In order to make the feds happy, we had to go back to the old price. Then we had to reduce the price of parts we sold below the old price by the same percentage we had increased the price. The price applied to all parts sold to any customer on a first-come basis until we had reached the volume we had sold at the increased price.

We, in effect, gave back any increase we'd received. It obviously didn't go back to the same customers in most cases. We also had to send all kinds of reports to the federal government. The dollar amount was almost insignificant, but the cost to comply cost both Lee Motors, Inc. and the federal government several hundred times the amount discounted to our customers.

This is typical government bureaucracy. It cost Lee Motors, Inc. money, and the cost to the federal government was a total waste of taxpayer money. Don't ever make the mistake of thinking your business is too small for *Big Brother* to notice.

Chapter 24: Creative Financing

Now, let's get into some creative financing. As a Ford-Mercury dealer in my twenties, I was the youngest individual in Ford's history to hold a franchise in his own name. There were younger dealers, but the actual franchises were held in an older relative's name.

As the son of a tenant farmer, I obviously had no family money. I was a graduate student with $1,000 in the bank and $1,000 equity in a car at the time.

How could I buy an automobile dealership, obtain the franchise, move to the town, and buy a home on the golf course? My mother said someone once asked her how I bought a car dealership. She responded, "He never said, and I never asked."

Buying the house on the golf course was the easy part, after I'd completed the deal for the Ford-Mercury dealership in town. I owned 50% of Lee Motors, Inc. I had a good salary with benefits and perks, like both my wife and I driving new cars. Financing 100% of the house wasn't a problem.

I financed Lee Motors, Inc. with silent investors. The mechanics involved an "S" corporation, common stock, and *Owners Notes to the Corporation*.

I had a friend who was the manager for a medical investment group that owned some medical properties and an X-ray clinic. That group of medical specialists was often looking for investments. This group made up the majority of my investors.

After looking at several automotive dealerships that were for sale in the area, I found one doing a terrible business, but I thought it had potential. Because of financial troubles, I could buy it at a fire sale price.

I got copies of the books and had a CPA go over them. For credibility, I used the same CPA the medical investment group used. I then set up a meeting with some of people from the medical investment group.

◆　◆　◆

Let's assume I needed $300,000 dollars from silent investors. That $300,000 would be loaned to the corporation. In exchange for the $300,000 in loans, the investors could buy $1,200 in common stock at $1 per share. I would then buy a matching $1,200 in common stock at $1 per share. Remember, $1,200 is about all the cash I could come up with at the time.

My friend, the manager for the medical investment group, committed for $50,000 in notes and $200 in common stock for a total investment of $50,200. One doctor committed for $150,000 in notes and $600 in common stock for a total investment of $150,600. Another doctor committed for $50,000 in notes and $200 in common stock for a total investment of $50,200. A neighbor of mine had expressed interest and wanted in for $50,000 in notes and $200 in common stock for a total investment of $50,200.

I now had verbal commitments from silent investors for $301,200. I made an offer on the business using my $1,000 cash for earnest money. The offer was accepted with a possession date of July 1, about ten weeks away.

I then had an attorney friend research the attorneys in the same town as the dealership and make a recommendation. I contacted that attorney to do the incorporation. I forget how long he said it would take, but I remember telling him any time at his convenience would be fine as long as we got it done before we closed and took possession. This was about one third the time he said he needed, but he made it happen with time to spare.

I then contacted one of the local banks and made arrangements for new car floorplan financing. I used the same bank as the one the existing dealer worked with. They were happy I only asked for financing for new vehicles, since the existing dealer floor-planned both new and used vehicles. He was obviously undercapitalized and in trouble financially.

◆ ◆ ◆

I also had to contact Ford Motor Company to approve the sale and award me the franchise. This turned out to be somewhat of a problem, being a twenty-six year-old kid with basically no automotive experience. I had no money, and my financing was creative to say the least. I had limited work experience and a good military record. I had a good education with a Bachelor of Business Administration degree and I would receive my MBA a month after I would take over the dealership.

No one at Ford would say yes or no all the way to the vice president who had the final approval. I was told he said, "I see why no one would say yes or no. I haven't ever seen anything like it. But, I haven't ever seen anyone with the guts to try it, so I'm going to approve it."

The only condition to awarding the franchise was that I move to new facilities on the highway within five years. The current location and facilities dated back to the Model A and were bad.

There were a few other details to deal with, like getting a new lease on the existing facility, obtaining insurance, buying a house, and moving to town before I took possession of the business. It's certainly good I was young and naïve or I never would have tried it.

◆   ◆   ◆

I'd like to give some more details of the financing. The investors had to make loans to the corporation to have the right to buy common stock. The common stock is in proportion to the loans to the corporation.

These *Owners Notes to the Corporation* were five-year loans; they could have been any term needed. The interest the notes paid should, in my opinion, be higher than current Certificates of Deposits. You and your investors have to make this decision. We paid interest on the notes annually.

We authorized a million shares of common stock, but only issued 2,400 shares. Please note the common stock ownership. I owned 1,200 shares and the four silent investors owned 1,200 shares between them. Management (me) owned 50%, and the silent investors owned 50%. I think this 50-50 split between management and investors is very important. I can hear some of you saying you want 51%. Trust me; you don't want 51%. I won't go into the details, but there are legal ramifications you don't want. Why would you need 51%? If you can't get one of your four silent investors to agree with you, you better think about it again anyway.

At our first stockholders meeting we elected all five stockholders to the Board of Directors, and I was elected Chairman. We elected the officers of the corporation including me as President.

◆　◆　◆

I would recommend a *Closed Corporation*. This means that the stock isn't sold to the public. Every year at the annual stockholders meeting we voted to set the value of the common stock.

If someone wanted to sell his or her stock, the price was already set. Our bylaws said the corporation first had the right to buy and retire the stock. If the corporation did not buy and retire the stock, the remaining stockholders had the right to buy the stock in proportion to their existing stock ownership.

Only after the corporation and all existing stockholders have refused the stock can the stock be sold to a new investor. The price of the stock would then be negotiable.

In the case of a husband and wife, the stock should typically be in both names. Lee Motors, Inc. had a stockholder die and his wife's name wasn't on the stock. She wanted to keep the stock. Technically, the corporation had to refuse to buy and retire the stock. Then all the other stockholders had to refuse to buy the stock for the wife to retain the stock. This is what we did.

◆　◆　◆

You also want to make sure the number of

investors is low enough so you are not subject to any Securities Exchange Commission regulations. The type and number of investors are a consideration. How these investors are solicited is also a consideration. Check with your specific state. Your attorney should also be of help in this area, especially if he or she understands securities laws.

Don't take your attorney's word as gospel with this innovative financing. The odds are that he or she has never been exposed to creative financing like this. I once interviewed attorneys for another business venture using the same type of financing in another state. Two out of three attorneys interviewed told me I couldn't do what I wanted. Of course, I knew better as I'd done it before. It made it pretty easy to make my selection, as only one understood what I wanted to do.

Always interview all professional people before you retain them. Not every attorney or CPA will be an expert in the areas you need help, as most professionals specialize. Find professions that provide the help you need. Some professional people only know one way to do things and are not open to new ideas. You don't need that kind of help either.

◆   ◆   ◆

I've just given you one example. It will not and does not fit all situations. It's simply meant to give you ideas for the creative financing you might need for your business.

I'd like to mention one more thing. *Keep It Simple Stupid*. For example, don't make your investor agreement so detailed and complicated that you scare them away.

I had my attorney draw up an investor agreement once, and he came back with an agreement fourteen legal pages long. I told him it was too long and too intimidating. I reworked the agreement into one 8 ½ x 11 page document. I gave it back to my attorney for his comments. He said it covered everything it needed to cover and approved it.

Legal considerations are a little like insurance. You can't cover every possible situation so remember the KISS principle.

Chapter 25: Independent Startup Business

If you're going to own your own business, you have basically four options available. They are:

1. Start an independent business from scratch

2. Buy an existing business

3. Buy a business opportunity

4. Buy a franchise

Let's look at independent startups first. By definition this means you are starting from nothing. You have no proven business system, and you're working independently with no help except the help you retain.

Some independent business startups are huge success stories. YouTube started with a few computers in a garage. They landed millions in venture capital in their first year, and sold to Google for $1.7 billion without ever making a profit. Please remember, this is the exception rather than the rule.

Today's Facebook story almost makes YouTube look like a failure. Don't count on this happening with your business.

Starting a business from scratch on your own sounds very romantic. Most start small with hopes of growing. This is one of the myths we talked about earlier. It may sound romantic and it may even be fun, but it's hard work and the chance of success is not very good.

The facts are, most independent business start-ups fail. I won't quote specific figures and studies, as they all vary depending on the time, place, and the sample group used for the study. My opinion is that over 80% of all independent startups can expect to fail before ten years. That's not very good.

Some specific businesses have even a higher failure rate. I know an individual who has a very successful business selling new and used restaurant equipment and supplies. It's such a good business because he sells equipment and supplies to new independent business startups. He sells on terms with substantial down payments. When the restaurant fails, he repossesses the equipment and supplies, and sells them again.

Most independent startups are not really new and innovative. Most are a variation on the businesses that will be the competition, or are just new to an area.

If your business is new to the area, you can probably expect competition almost immediately. You do not and will not have a monopoly. If there is good demand for your product or service, you will have competition.

How will your business be different from the competition? How are you going to distinguish your product or service from the competition? If your business is a variation on a business, is that variation something that will make the business successful?

What will your market niche be? There are

probably dozens of ways you can differentiate your business from your competition. Advertising, convenience, delivery, image, location, people, price, promotions, quality, selection, service, and speed are a few.

You know my opinion of competing on price. If you plan to compete on price, make sure you'll be able to cover your expenses and show a profit?

♦   ♦   ♦

As a car dealer, I had a good friend who was a Firestone tire dealer. John became a dealer in the early '70s when a tire franchise was what I call a product franchise. At that time, Firestone gave the franchisee the right to use the name and logo. They also agreed to sell him product. That's about it. The dealer was then on his own, almost like starting any other business from scratch. Today, a Firestone tire franchise would provide the franchisee with a complete business system.

John had worked for a Goodyear tire dealer in the same town for many years and knew the business. He had a good business plan and system. John worked in a rural community and did a lot of business with farm implement and truck tires. He knew his customer and how he would compete. He sometimes joked that he sold a $200 tire for $100, but he would to make it up on volume.

John operated out of a retail facility that should have been condemned years before. John became friends with most of his customers. He kept the coffee hot. The front office had a piece of plywood on top of a stack of tires for playing cards. There were several old kitchen chairs that didn't match around the *card table*. A farmer didn't have any problem stopping in with his dirty boots.

John knew the value of providing the needed tire with quick service to his customers. John made every effort to have the tires his customers needed in stock.

I once saw one of John's customers negotiating price on some farm tractor tires. The customer said the Goodyear dealer had a better price. John asked if the Goodyear dealer had the tires in stock. When the farmer said no, John said he would sell the tires for that price too, if he didn't have them. The customer laughed and said, "Put them on."

As a car dealer, I sometimes traded for or bought a used car that needed tires. If I went to the other tire dealers in town, they were always trying to sell me the top of the line tires at a premium price.

John understood I needed good-looking, new rubber on the car to sell it. He would mount new tires of a quality and look warranted for the vehicle. He would bubble balance the tires with used weights at no charge. I'd get maximum value for the dollar and get a saleable vehicle.

John knew what I wanted. I didn't need to negotiate every tire purchase. I could have a porter drop the used car off at John's business, and he would take care of it.

John and I also traded business. He charged the tires I bought to an open account. I usually owed him a lot of money. John bought his vehicles from me so we would eventually settle up the account. One time John told me he wanted a late model, loaded Mercury station wagon for his wife. I didn't have any, but told him I would keep my eyes open for one.

One Saturday, John visited a neighboring town on business and saw a year-old Mercury station wagon at one of my friendly Ford and Mercury competitors that we'll call Bob. John told Bob he wanted the vehicle, but had to buy it from me. John asked Bob if he would wholesale the car to me, and Bob said fine.

Bob said he had to come to the courthouse in my town on Monday anyway so he would deliver the car to me then. On Monday morning, Bob stopped at my dealership with the Mercury wagon. He informed me I was buying it to sell to John. Since this was the first I'd heard about it, I asked Bob if I'd made a good deal.

I once lost a car to John in a poker game. This is not as bad as it sounds. I'd traded for an old junk Mercury Comet convertible. Only about four of the six cylinders were firing. I'd appraised the car from the showroom window and told the salesman to value it at whatever the wheel covers were worth.

The Comet had been sitting on the back lot when I wanted an old beater convertible for some reason. I got it started, and put the top down. I never bothered to put the top up again. If it rained, it rained, and I'd waited for it to dry out.

One night at the country club, I was light on a pot, and John said he would take the Comet *as-is* for what I was light on the pot if I lost. I lost the poker hand and John got the Comet convertible.

My point is that John knew the tire business. He knew his customer. He knew what his customer wanted and how to service that customer. He knew the image he wanted to project.

John knew what it would cost to start and operate his business. John had a business plan and business system. He made sure he had adequate capital to have the tires his customer needed in stock for immediate delivery. He ran a business with a unique image, and he was successful.

John knew his market niche. He knew his customer and made every effort to serve that customer's needs. He also knew he couldn't be everything to everybody, and didn't make that mistake.

◆ ◆ ◆

I need to define what I mean by a business plan vs. a business system. A business plan is usually a brief description of the business and some financial projections.

A business system is much more. A business system is a detailed description of everything needed to successfully operate a business. This will include all products and services offered. The customer will be defined. A complete marketing program will be spelled out in detail. Personnel, job descriptions, and training will be included in the business system. Anything important to starting and operating the business will be included in the written business system.

It's very important your business system be written and not just in your head. You won't get the business system right the first time. It will always be changing, but the more you have, the better. Computers and word processing are great for changing the business system as you learn. Hopefully, you have enough experience in the industry so you're not totally reinventing the wheel. Once you start operations, you won't have time to be writing it from scratch.

◆   ◆   ◆

Ideally, you'll have experience in the industry before starting a business from scratch. Competing in business is hard enough when you have a proven business system. You must have enough experience in the industry you're starting your business to develop and implement a good business system.

Be careful if you are starting a business in the same industry you now work and have a *Non-Compete Agreement*. You don't need the trouble of a lawsuit while you are starting a business.

I know an individual associated with a non-profit economic development organization in Wisconsin who we'll call Jill. Jill says she has several people a month approach her about opening a sporting goods store specializing in hunting and fishing equipment. When she asks them about their experience, they respond that they have hunted and fished all their life. When Jill asks them how they'll attract customers, they respond that they have a lot of friends that say they'll do business with them.

Jill now knows this business is almost sure to fail. Her client has no clue about running a retail store, much less a sporting goods store specializing in hunting and fishing. She knows that the client doesn't have enough friends to support the business. She also knows that many of the friends will also only use him as their exclusive supplier as long as he has what they want and gives them a deal. Many friends will expect to get their purchases at cost. After all, they are friends.

Jill now has to talk them out of starting this business. If she can't do that, she has to try to educate them so they research the business properly. She has to push them to develop a business plan and business system. She doesn't want them to fail and lose their investment if she can help it.

Jill also commented about people wanting to start coffee shops. She said people thought this would be a fun business, and would say, "How hard can it be to run a coffee shop?" The client often had some particular flavors that they like much better than Starbucks. They don't even consider that the general public might not prefer those flavors. If there were a strong demand for these flavors, Starbucks would probably already be offering them.

Jill said she's seen several coffee shops that have opened and closed in about three months. Sometimes even in the same location with different decors and different owners. Each new owner was sure that their decorating, their favorite flavors, and the support of their friends would make them successful. Unfortunately, it just didn't work that way.

◆ ◆ ◆

As a general rule, most independent business start-ups cannot compete with larger chain and franchise operations. I wouldn't recommend even considering trying to compete with these chain and franchise operations. You'll probably fail. Find a niche market and work that market.

This may mean you'll run a smaller operation with lower overhead that's hopefully cost effective. As a small independent, you cannot afford mass advertising to promote your business. You'll need to promote your business with guerrilla marketing as we discussed in the marketing chapter.

These small independent operations will sometimes be nothing more than a way to create a job. In these cases you'll not only be the owner and manager, but the technician or sales clerk providing the service to your customer. You may be the only employee of your business.

People from the trades or people with specialized skills do quite well with small, specialized businesses. You may be the best in your field, but don't make the mistake of thinking this is enough to be successful. You still need to market your business.

This type of independent business is good if it meets your goals and needs. You'll probably never get rich, but it may provide you with the lifestyle you want. Many of these businesses are started with an investment of under $10,000.

◆ ◆ ◆

An independent business start-up requires a lot more than just prior experience in the business and a good business system. Among other things, you need to determine if there's a market for your product or service. You probably need professional help in several areas, and the business must be properly financed.

How do you determine if there's enough of a market demand for your business to make it successful? This is a tough one. As we previously discussed, good market research will be very expensive, and is probably not cost effective for a small independent business start-up. Doing your own market research may be difficult and may not provide accurate results, as it's hard to keep personal emotions and perceptions out of your conclusions.

You'll also need to hire professional consultants or employees in every area you are not proficient. Some of these areas are sales, marketing, advertising, real estate, facility design, facility build-out, accounting, financing, legal, incorporation, insurance, taxes, human resources, and anything else relevant to your specific business. No one can be an expert in all areas. You probably also cannot afford to hire professionals in all areas, so you'll have to decide what's most essential and cost effective.

As I previously mentioned, Professor Vaughan once said that if you buy insurance to cover every possible risk, it would bankrupt you. This is true in almost every area of business. You can't afford to investigate, anticipate, and have a plan to deal with every possible contingency.

◆　◆　◆

You need to make sure you've adequately financed your small business start-up. It's pretty easy to compute this. Make a list of every expense you can think of to start the business. Include the professionals listed above. Don't forget a general operating slush fund.

You also need to include your salary or living expenses until the business turns a profit. How long will it take to build the new business so it will provide you with the income you want out of the business? Estimates of one year to five years are not unusual for a business to be profitable. You may need to add up the five years of living expenses for yourself into the initial capitalization for the business.

The second step is to increase every cost to what you think is the maximum. Next, increase every cost to cover a maximum time to reach profitability you need or want. I guarantee many things will take twice as long as you think they should. Plan for it.

Now that you have every possible cost at the maximum highest cost with the longest maximum time delay, get a total dollar amount for the project. Now *DOUBLE IT*. You will still be short, but it'll be close.

◆ ◆ ◆

Obviously, I don't feel most people should do an independent business start-up. The chances of success aren't good compared to a franchise, but the facts are that every successful franchise today, to the best of my knowledge, started out as a single independent business start-up.

Small independent businesses without employees seem to have a better chance of success as they're just creating a job. You won't get rich, but it may fit your needs and meet your goals. The chances of getting rich by being in business for yourself is not very likely anyway.

If you're considering starting a business from scratch, make sure you have experience in the industry, do your homework, and make sure you're adequately capitalized. Good luck. As the saying goes, "It's better to be lucky than good."

Chapter 26: Buy an Existing Business

Buying an existing business sounds very attractive to most people considering self-employment for the first time. I think this is especially true of people coming out of the corporate world.

What they're looking for is pretty simple. They want a proven, established business that's profitable. They want to buy a business that can provide them immediate income. They'd also like to buy the business on some kind of contract terms with the seller carrying the contract, so the buyer doesn't have to invest much cash initially. This sounds good. It's too bad that the business described does not exist.

If this business did exist, the chances are it wouldn't be in the paper or listed by a business broker. A son, daughter, relative, employee, employees, or even a business broker would have already bought the business. Yes, business brokers do sometimes keep the best deals for themselves.

If a good business is listed with a business broker, the first thing most brokers do is contact the competitors of the business. Mergers and acquisitions is big business in this country. This is the only thing some business brokers do, and why not? Selling to a competitor is much easier than finding a new buyer. The broker can identify the competitors and contact them much easier than trying to find a new buyer.

A competitor also knows the industry and knows

how to evaluate the business. This is much easier than having to educate a buyer that isn't familiar with the industry.

◆　◆　◆

Looking for this ideal business reminds me of a potential customer who called me when I worked in the collector car business. This potential customer called looking for a 1970 Chevelle SS convertible with a 4-speed transmission and a LS6 engine. The 1970 Chevelle is a popular muscle car.

LS6 is the factory code for a solid lifter, V-8 engine with 454 CID (Cubic Inch Displacement). The engine was rated at 450 horsepower, but some people feel the engine actually produced over 500 horsepower. It is fun to drive.

The customer wanted the car to be red with tan interior. He wanted a #2 quality car, but he would take a #1 quality car. A #2 quality car is the highest quality car you would drive. A #1 car is a show car that is hauled around on a trailer and not driven.

The customer wanted the car to be *Correct,* meaning it would have the same colors and equipment as when originally built. He wanted the original *Build Sheet* to verify the car's specs. The build sheet is a production paper listing the colors and equipment for the car when built. The build sheet could usually be found attached to the underside of the rear seat cushion when this model left the factory.

The customer also wanted a numbers matching car. This meant it had the original engine and transmission. These would have the VIN (Vehicle Identification Number) for the vehicle stamped on the engine block and transmission case.

The customer even wanted an original car that had not been restored. To find any unrestored thirty-year-old car in #2 condition would be a find. To find an unrestored thirty-year-old muscle car in #2 would be a miracle. Muscle cars were bought to drive hard and race. I personally drove new Pontiac GTOs from 1965 to 1969. Of course, I didn't drive mine hard, and if you believe that, someone is going to sell you something like a bridge.

Let's get back to the 1970 Chevelle. Most experts agree there were less than twenty 1970 Chevelle SS convertibles made with LS6 engines. There is some disagreement as to the exact number, but there were probably seventeen to nineteen built.

If there were less than twenty built, how many were built with red paint, tan interior, and a 4-speed? Probably none, and if there were any built, the odds of it remaining an unrestored, numbers matching car would be infinitesimal.

I tried to explain to the customer that the car he described probably didn't exist. I also explained that if this car did exist, it would probably sell for an astronomical price.

The customer told me in a huffy manner that these cars were out there, and he could by them for $20,000. I politely asked him to please let me know if he found any extra at that price.

I know an individual who has a full-time business making correct, numbers matching, 1970 SS Chevelles with LS6 engines. He re-stamps engine blocks and transmission cases with matching VINs. He forges the needed documentation and sells the clones for good money. The customer I was talking about is his prey.

My point is an uninformed individual who has not done his homework is the prey of unscrupulous people in any industry. There's a saying, "If it sounds too good to be true, it probably is." Do your research.

If you are looking for an established, profitable business that will provide you immediate income that you can buy on terms, it probably does not exist. Accept it. Now we can start over.

◆　◆　◆

If you want an established and proven business that can provide you with immediate income, you'll pay for it. These businesses are few and far between. When they do come on the market, they command a premium price with a lot of *Blue Sky* included in the price. The sellers and/or the business brokers offering these businesses won't have to make any excuses for these businesses.

Blue Sky is the portion of the purchase price that can't be explained by anything tangible. Many things might explain and justify the blue sky included in the price. A recognized name, logo, or brand might justify blue sky. A loyal, trained, efficient, and productive group of employees might command a premium price. A loyal customer base might command a premium price. There are a lot of other things that add value to a business, but aren't tangible. You must expect to pay for these intangibles with hard cash.

◆　◆　◆

If you're looking for an existing business and don't have the resources to pay for blue sky, you'll have to buy a business that's not doing quite so well. This will probably mean you will not be able to take money out of the business until you build the business up. You'll have to budget for what you need to live on until the business can provide it.

When I bought the Ford-Mercury dealership I didn't pay for any blue sky as the dealership had been losing money for years. I didn't pay a premium, but I did take a gamble that I could turn the business around. If I couldn't turn the business around, I could have lost all my investment and the investment of my silent investors.

Buying the car dealership was a big gamble. I certainly wasn't stupid, but I was young and naïve or I might not have done it. When I think about buying the dealership now, I realize how big a gamble I made.

◆　◆　◆

When you consider buying a business that's not at its peak, everyone representing the business including the seller and/or the business broker will make excuses for the business. They'll talk about all the potential the business has. You must ask yourself why the business isn't doing better if it has so much potential. Why is the owner really selling the business?

You'll hear all kinds of excuses; here are some of the most popular: The owner is getting ready to retire; the owner has health problems; the owner is getting a divorce; the owner has lost interest in the business. Any of these and others directly related to the owner could be true. Even if they are true, this means the business is dependent on the owner to be profitable. It's not a business that will run with minimal management.

The owner and the management will be you if you buy the business. Can you make a difference?

What's the business's market niche? Will you keep the same niche or will you change it? Be very careful making changes. If you make major changes, you may attract new customers, but you may lose current customers.

As I mentioned, I live on a chain of lakes in Wisconsin. There are several restaurants and bars located on this chain of lakes. Owning a restaurant on a lake in a resort and vacation area sounds like a lot of fun, doesn't it?

Some of these restaurants have changed owners in the few years we've lived here. Some have changed owners several times. Why?

The restaurant business is a tough, competitive business. If you go into this business, you better have a lot of experience in the restaurant business, or have an experienced manager, or have a proven and tight business system to follow.

This is what happened in most of the restaurant sales on our chain of lakes: The new owner had no restaurant experience; they made a lot of changes fast; they spent, or in most cases, wasted a lot or money on changes. Business dropped off; they were soon losing a lot of money and were forced to sell at a loss.

When one of the restaurants was sold we learned that a couple we knew had gotten involved. This couple would be the new managers of the restaurant and were minor investors in the business.

This restaurant did a good business and made money. The restaurant had an excellent reputation for several things including a Bloody Mary with a lot of garnishes and a beer chaser. Deep fried cheese curds were another specialty. Both were a couple of my favorites. The first time I saw the couple, I jokingly warned them about changing the Bloody Mary or the fried cheese curds. They assured me the only changes made would be improvements.

When the new owners took over, they closed down for several weeks to make needed renovations and give it a good cleaning. Both were definitely needed, but I'm not sure shutting down was necessary or good for the business.

When they reopened the menu had completely changed. The first time I stopped, I ordered a Bloody Mary. It tasted bad and didn't have the expected garnishes. They no longer offered fried cheese curds on the menu. The new menu had been designed by one of the manager's sons, a student at a chef school. The menu might have been great in an exclusive metropolitan area, but remember this is a northern Wisconsin resort area.

The restaurant never made a profit for the new owners. Soon the owner/managers were gone. Absentee owners were now running it with little chance for success. Soon after, the kitchen shut down leaving just the bar.

The restaurant has now been sold again. This time the owners have some restaurant experience. I hope they'll be successful.

◆ ◆ ◆

Another example is a golf course and bar in my area that changed owners. The new owners had neither golf course nor bar experience.

With the previous owners, the pro shop was located in the same building as the bar. In slow times the bartender also handled the tee times, green fees, and pro shop. This wasn't an ideal situation, but labor efficient.

The new owners converted one of the maintenance buildings into a pro shop. This created additional labor costs, as the bartender could no longer handle it.

Next, the new owners put a fence around the bar patio and built a stage. They tried to create a tiki bar with live entertainment. The patio wasn't on the water. It didn't even face the golf course.

This is a resort area with a relatively low population. The demographics of the area are more retirement age than kids. Any experienced bar manager doing any market research would have known that the tiki bar could never draw enough business to pay for the band let alone make a profit.

They hired a band a few times to play for the new owners. I hope they enjoyed it as they'd made a major capital expenditure that will never give any return on investment.

If you buy an existing business, be very careful before making changes. Do your market research. Don't make changes based on your personal preferences.

Both the golf course and the bar have now been sold again. The new owners of the golf course actually have golf course experience. The new owners of the bar actually have restaurant and bar experience. I hope both do well.

♦ ♦ ♦

There are many reasons why a business may not be doing well.

There may be new competition. Talk to the competition. There may have been changes in personnel with the business. Maybe traffic patterns have changed so the location is no longer good. Maybe the business had quit or changed its marketing or advertising. We could go on almost indefinitely, but you get the idea. Why has the business declined?

A change in the market or a change in the demand for the product or service is a possibility that should always be considered. Before the gasoline engine, horses were a major part of this country's economy. The harness making business was a good business. That business has changed. Many companies that made horse harnesses went out of business, and those that survived have adapted to new and different customers.

Every business has a life cycle that usually resembles the bell curve. Demand will be very low at first. Demand will then increase slowly at first and then quite rapidly until it reaches its peak. Once demand approaches the top of the bell curve it slows down and then starts to decline. Demand will then drop quite quickly, until it starts to level off at a very low demand to no demand at all.

The life cycle for every product or service is different. Some are long and some are short. Horses played an important role for centuries prior to the gasoline engine. The hula-hoop's life cycle had a very short peak demand.

There are no guarantees. Some products and

services will have a long life cycle and some are just a fad that will fade quickly. Just be aware that nothing is forever. Ideally, we want a business with a long life cycle where the demand for our product or service is on the up side of the bell curve and not the down side.

◆　◆　◆

How do you evaluate a business? This is a good question that's critical to your decision to buy the business. The first and most important thing is to not get overly excited about the product or service. The fact that you like or use the product personally should not be a major part of your evaluation. Your personal opinion of the product or service may not be representative of the marketplace. Evaluating a product or service based on your personal likes or dislikes is making a decision on emotion and personal perception.

I once heard of an individual who made a small fortune selling his business. This business consistently lost money. The business involved a product that had a very attractive image and a hobby for a lot of people. People with this hobby perceived the business as fun with a lot of potential demand and profit. Neither true in actuality.

The original owner sold the business on contract with substantial down payments. When the new owners realized how much money they were losing with the business, they would default on the contract, and let the business go back to the original owner. The original owner sold this *fun* business with substantial down payments several times and always got the business back when the new owners defaulted on the contract. The new owner had eventually received down payments in excess of the businesses total value and he still owned the business. By the way, the business never made any money. Be very careful of *fun* businesses.

Look at the books. This is an obvious part of evaluating a business. You probably want professional help with this. A CPA will see things you may miss. If the business is large, an independent firm may have audited the books. This is good, but still have your own people look at the books.

If the business you're looking at is a franchise, the franchisor may demand a standardized accounting system, which is good. An independent business may take liberties with the books. Be careful. Enron is not the only business that knows how to cook the books. They were just big and got caught.

Looking at the books gives you a good history of the company. Remember, there's no guarantee that the business will do the same in the future. You'll have to make that decision. Look at trends. Have sales and profits increased or decreased in recent years?

One advantage of being a small independent business owner is that you have a lot of flexibility on the benefits you pay yourself. Sometimes these perks to the owner are a way of reducing earnings and avoiding taxes. The problem is identifying these perks or benefits, and determining if they're legal.

Some small business owners skim money from their business to avoid taxes. Since this is not legal, there is no way you can verify this income. Hopefully, most reputable business owners will show all income for several years before selling their business so you can realistically evaluate the business. If the owner claims to have skimmed money from the business, there's no way to verify this. You're forced to take his or her word. Do you want to trust the word of a tax cheat? Buyer beware!

When evaluating a business, ask if there's a business system and if that system is in writing. Are there job descriptions and are they in writing? What outside support and training are available? If you're buying a business that's a good franchise, all of these things should be in place.

If the business is independent, none of these may be present. You now have to determine how much of the business is dependent on the existing owner? Will the customers stay when the current owner leaves? Will the employees stay when he or she leaves?

If the business is highly dependent on the existing owner, will he or she stay on to help with the transition? How long do you want them to stay? How long do they want to stay? What compensation do they want?

◆ ◆ ◆

Some sellers want to keep the fact that they are selling the business confidential. This isn't necessarily a negative. It may be necessary to keep the confidence of customers and employees.

If you're allowed the opportunity to talk to employees, please take advantage it. You need to talk to them on a one-on-one situation without the owner or business broker being present. You don't need to talk to every employee, but talk to a good sample. The employees know the business and may give you a totally different perspective than the owners and business broker.

In Chapter four, "Why Own Your Own Business," I gave an example of my boss driving me crazy. You may remember how the consultant told me that I had a problem with the owner in the corner office, and how I had to find some way to keep him out of the daily operations.

The owner had started the very well capitalized business with family money. His strengths were being a tenacious salesman, and hiring good people. After all, he hired me.

Unfortunately, he'd never made money in any two consecutive years until the last six years after I'd been named General Manager. Our CPA for the firm always wanted to defer income in profitable years as the next year would probably lose money, but we continued to make money every year.

We had made the business the clear leader in the industry, and we'd made a lot of money for six years straight. Too bad the business had grown beyond where the owner could really understand or run the business.

The business sold. The new owners bought it without talking to any of the employees, including me. They never knew why the business had become an industry leader, or why it made money.

The new owners felt they could do my job as general manager cheaper and better, so they let me go. Sources told me they lost money for years. I don't know if this is true, but I do know their image has changed, and a lot of people have been let go. One source told me, "They are burning the furniture to stay warm."

What a shame. Talking to the employees, and in this case, the general manager could have prevented this huge financial mistake. Employees will be guarded with what they say, but you should be able to read between the lines.

If you were considering buying the business and never talked to anyone except the owner and/or the business broker, you would have no clue what is happening with the business or why. This is why you need to talk to employees and managers if possible.

I highly recommend talking to more people than just the selling owner and business broker. This includes employees of the business, and people outside the business that are familiar with the business. It's just possible the selling owner and/or business broker will puff the description of the business. I'm not saying they illegally represent the business, but they can certainly make it look more attractive than it is.

In some cases, misrepresentation may even be to the point of fraud. Try to avoid these situations. While it's true you might have recourse in the courts, it hardly ever works out well. The only people who make money are the attorneys.

◆　◆　◆

Buying a collector car sight unseen is not that unusual in the business. With eighty percent of all the collector cars I have sold, the buyer didn't see the car until delivery. You must be able to trust the person you're buying the car from, or get an independent appraisal.

I once had an individual hire me to appraise a collector car for him. He lived in the Chicago area and had bought the car sight unseen in Florida. Before he bought it, he'd hired an appraiser who was a friend of the seller, and recommended by the seller to appraise the car. Sounded like a potential problem to me.

The seller had described the car, a 1962 Oldsmobile Starfire convertible, as a correct, numbers matching car in number two condition. As described, the retail value of the car at that time would have been about $22,000. It would be much higher today. The owner had priced the car for $12,000, so it sounded like a good deal, or was it too good to be true?

The written appraisal never actually described the car in the terms the owner had used. The appraisal went into great detail describing many insignificant details. For example, the appraisal stated the glove box liner did not look original. The appraiser said nothing incorrect or fraudulent, but he certainly didn't describe the car. The buyer got so excited about the car and the potential *deal* that he overlooked that the appraisal didn't really describe the car.

When I first saw the car, I didn't even want to do the appraisal. The owner insisted, saying he knew he'd been cheated. He just wanted to know how badly.

The car was a 1962 Oldsmobile Starfire coupe that had the top cut off and a convertible top installed. The convertible top mechanism wasn't even power. Not only did the car not have the original engine, but it didn't even have a correct engine for a Starfire. The car was a lot rougher than number two condition, probably number three at best, or more realistically a number four. The brushed stainless body side trim was in excellent condition and the only redeeming feature of the car. This trim is valuable.

The buyer had paid $12,000 for the car. I think I appraised it at $2,500. The buyer had been cheated, probably to the point of fraud. The buyer could take the seller to court, but jurisdiction would probably have to be in Florida, and it would be expensive. If he ever did get a judgment, it might take years, and he then might never be able to collect.

Be careful where you get your information. Talk to more than one or two sources, and don't take things at face value.

◆　◆　◆

The most important consideration when evaluating a business is what your role in the business will be. What will your daily duties include? Will you be happy performing your daily tasks? If you're not happy in your role, your chances of success are much lower.

What were the duties of the previous owner? Will your duties be the same as the previous owner? If not, you'll have to make changes in personnel or hire new personnel. For example, if the previous owner handled the sales and you don't like to sell, you'll need to hire a sales manager.

Industry knowledge may not be as critical when buying an existing business as when starting from scratch, but it's still very important. If you're not familiar with the industry, learn everything you can about the industry. It's almost impossible to evaluate the future of a business if you don't know the industry. It's also essential the complete business system be in writing if you're not familiar with the industry.

Please note that I never mentioned the product or service. It's just not important compared to what your daily activities are. Focus on what's important for reaching your goals.

Chapter 27: Business Opportunities

For the purposes of this book, I'll define a *Business Opportunity* as any business that's not an existing business, a new independent start-up, or a franchise. There are a lot of good business opportunities. I've occasionally recommended a client investigate a business opportunity. Unfortunately, many are just scams. Business opportunities are basically unregulated and hard to validate.

There are all kinds of business opportunities. Some are Internet businesses, work-at-home businesses, distributorships, route sales, service businesses and multi-level marketing. Many business opportunity models are simply you working alone as an independent contractor.

◆　◆　◆

Let's take a look at some of the opportunities involving the Internet. The YouTube story previously mentioned is unique and not likely to repeat often. Let's take a look at a more likely result.

I had a client who we'll call Dean. Dean had invested in an Internet shopping web site with a simple idea. Local businesses could market their goods on the site. The shopper would type in their zip code and shop for the desired product from local suppliers. The idea sounds simple enough, and there should be a demand for the service.

After over two million dollars spent on

development, the founder declared bankruptcy. Luckily, Dean had only invested about thirty thousand. Dean got all rights to the site signed over to him and kept it up for over two years with the idea of selling it to some other Internet company for the tax loss carryover. This never happened and the site shut down.

This scenario happens many times over for every success story. Don't let stars and dollar signs cloud your vision.

There are a lot of different opportunities involving the Internet. Some people do quite well buying e-mail lists and sending out various advertisements. These advertisements promote and sell all sorts of products.

E-mail marketing promotes almost every type of product, service and opportunity imaginable. There are a lot of programs to block this junk mail. I find these e-mails quite annoying myself.

There are many Internet business opportunities promising large incomes and quick riches. Besides the money, most of these Internet opportunities promise a great lifestyle. They say you can work your own hours from your own home with no boss. Most are just selling a gimmick to the gullible.

Some of these work-at-home computer business opportunities can provide some supplemental income. Few will ever provide a good living wage.

◆　◆　◆

Not all work-at-home business opportunities involve the Internet. Many of these can be home-based businesses.

A home-based business might be as simple as stuffing envelopes for direct mail. This type of business can provide some supplemental income with great flexibility in work hours. On the negative side, you may not make minimum wage. This is legal as you'll be in business for yourself as an independent contractor.

Telemarketing is another business opportunity that can often be done from home. No, the do-not-call lists have not stopped the telemarketing industry. You must be able to handle the high rejection you'll experience in this business. You'll not totally set the hours you work, as you have to call when you can reach people. You'll be paid on performance so your income will vary. Again, you may not even make minimum wage.

◆ ◆ ◆

There are many kinds of business opportunities. Many are legitimate business opportunities, but most people buying the business opportunity will fail because they do not know how, or are not willing, to do what it takes to market their business.

The medical billing business is a perfect example. This can be a good business. There are a lot of people making six figure incomes in medical billing.

Often people think it's something they can do and buy the software and training to perform the medical billing function. They may be very capable of providing the medical billing service. The problem is that they need to market their service in order to get clients. This is where a majority will fail.

They'll make calls on medical offices and clinics in their area. They'll probably not get any clients on the first call. Some people will give up on the business at this point, without ever having a client.

Remember, the company that's selling you the software and training to do the medical billing are probably also trying to sell to the clinics and offices that are your potential clients. These healthcare providers can then perform the medical billing operation with in-house staff.

Some people will often continue marketing their service until they get some business. They'll seldom continue to market their service aggressively enough to secure enough business to provide the income they need. They will eventually give up on the business.

◆   ◆   ◆

Distributor business opportunities are attractive to many people. Some of these are very good, and some are not so good.

Soft drink bottlers hired independent contractors to distribute their product in the past. Some of these independent contractors made large incomes. Distribution for most of these products has now been taken over by the bottler using their own employees. The bottler has greater control and less cost using company trucks and employees.

There are still good opportunities in this type of business. For example, Pepperidge Farm still uses independent contractors to distribute some of their products, including cookies. Many people owning these routes do very well, but they must work the business and service their customers. A good route will bring a premium price.

Talk to other people doing the business to determine what is needed to be successful. Will you be happy with your day-to-day role in the business? Will it meet your needs?

◆ ◆ ◆

I once had a client who found a distributor opportunity in his local newspaper. It involved supplying fresh fruit to convenience stores. The business opportunity excited him.

I kept asking him to talk to other distributors in the business. He responded, "This is a great ground floor opportunity and he didn't need to talk to anyone else."

He contacted me about a year later. He said he wished he'd listened to me. His refrigerated delivery vehicle had been repossessed, his house was in foreclosure, and he needed a job. These stories break my heart, when most can be avoided if we can just keep our emotions and perceptions out of our decision making process.

◆ ◆ ◆

Multi-level marketing is another business opportunity that's always around. With multi-level marketing, you make money on what you sell, but the big opportunity is that you can set other people up in the business. These people will be your *down-line distributors* and you'll make a smaller percentage on what they sell.

There are many multi-level marketing companies. Some have been around for many years and will continue to be around for many more. Amway is an example of a strong and reputable multi-level company.

Some multi-level companies rise to great prominence and then almost disappear. One that fits this image, in my opinion, is Herbalife. In the late seventies, Herbalife was a boom company with phenomenal growth. Some distributors for Herbalife were making a fortune. Herbalife held a rally in Chicago that filled McCormick Place. Everyone wanted to sign up as many distributors as possible and get rich.

Herbalife had an excellent product. The problem was that most of their distributors just wanted to sign up more distributors. Nobody focused on selling the product. Some distributors weren't selling any product.

Herbalife did great for a while. When they recognized the problem, they changed their policy. They required every distributor to sell some minimum amount of product at retail in order to collect their percentage for their down-line distributors. Good idea, but it came too late.

Herbalife is still around today, but has never reached the level of the late seventies. Maybe this is good. Maybe they're a better company today. Who knows?

◆　◆　◆

Some multi-level companies do very well. People who get in early can do very well, if the company continues to thrive. Someone with a multi-level marketing business owns the largest house on the chain of lakes where I live. We sometimes refer to it as *The Palace.*

Be very careful of the hype surrounding *hot* multi-level companies in your area at any point in time. Most come and go. Validating a business opportunity is very hard. Most business opportunities won't give you a list of other people who have purchased their opportunity.

The names they do give you are the people who are the star performers. Talk to as many other people doing the same business opportunity as possible. Try to talk to some who have failed in the business so you can determine why they failed. It may be hard to locate these people with most business opportunities.

With multi-level marketing opportunities, talk to people in the business other than your *up-line*. Your *up-line* is trying to sell you on the opportunity so they can make their percentage off the product you sell. They really don't care if you succeed or make the income you need. Just signing up distributors won't work long-term if no one ever sells the product or service.

Please don't get caught up in the hype over the product or service. Determine what your role in the business will be. What will your responsibilities be on a day-to-day basis to make the business a success? Will you be happy in this role?

Selling business opportunities can be a good business if you like selling. You also must be morally comfortable knowing that a large majority of the people buying the business will fail, or at least not be successful.

Once in a previous life, I sold a medical billing business opportunity. I told my prospects they would fail if they didn't devote the time and effort to market their business.

The people selling and promoting a business opportunity are often more successful and make more money than the people actually working the business opportunity. Remember that someone has to sell the product or service if the business is going to be successful in the long run.

Chapter 28: Franchise Definition

If the material covered so far in this book is intimidating or overwhelming, maybe a franchise is an option you should consider. It's almost impossible for anyone to be an expert in every area needed when starting a business. That's why franchising is so successful.

I'll spend more time on franchising than other self-employment or investment options for three reasons:

1. I'm quite familiar with franchising.

2. I find franchising is very misunderstood.

3. Franchising offers a lot of options and has an excellent chance of offering a good option for many people looking for an investment or self-employment.

Franchising is a distribution system and/or a marketing concept. Franchising is not an industry. Franchising is probably the most successful distribution system or marketing concept in the world, but many people don't understand what or how it works.

◆　◆　◆

A distribution system is legally a franchise if:

1. The franchisor provides a common name, logo, and trademark to be used by the franchisee.

2. The franchisor provides a proven business system for the franchisee.

3. The franchisor provides initial and ongoing training and support.

4. The franchisee pays an initial fee and continuing fees to the franchisor.

If these four elements or conditions are present, a distribution system is legally a franchise regardless of what it may be called. If these four elements or conditions are not present, the distribution system is legally probably not a franchise regardless of what it is called.

◆　◆　◆

Theoretically, a franchise should give someone the opportunity to do something he or she can't do on their own. This is probably true in most cases, but is somewhat of a contradiction as to the best of my knowledge every franchise in existence today had at least one successful business operation before the business concept and business system was franchised.

The International Franchise Association says there are over 5,500 franchises in over 80 industries. As many as 300 new concepts are franchised every year. Franchising is involved in more than just fast food.

As with many things, franchising was basically unregulated for many years. This led to abuse by some franchisors. By 1970 franchising probably had more regulation than anything in the country. It is regulated by both the federal government and individual states.

The federal government requires that a prospective franchisee must be provided with a Uniform Franchise Offering Circular. This document is often referred to as a UFOC or disclosure document. This document must be provided to a franchisee at the appropriate time. The latest a UFOC can be given to a prospective franchisee is at the first face-to-face meeting with the franchisor. The prospective franchisee must have this document for a minimum of ten business days prior to signing any franchise agreements.

◆   ◆   ◆

The federal government requires twenty-three items be covered in the Uniform Franchise Offering Circular. They are:

1. The franchisor, its predecessors and affiliates

2. Business experience

3. Litigation

4. Bankruptcy

5. Initial franchise fees

6. Other fees

7. Initial Investment

8. Restrictions on sources of products and services

9. Franchisee's obligations

10. Financing

11. Franchisor's obligations

12. Territory

13. Trademarks

14. Patents, copyrights and proprietary information

15. Obligation to participate in the actual operation of the franchise business

16. Restrictions on what the franchisee may sell

17. Renewal, termination, transfer and dispute resolution

18. Public figures

19. Earnings claims

20. List of franchisees

21. Financial statements

22. Contracts

23. Receipt for Uniform Franchise Offering Circular

The Federal Government doesn't require the UFCO to be filed with any government agency. Thirty-five states have no additional requirement to sell franchises in the state concerning disclosure statements, or filings with the state.

Fifteen states require the Uniform Franchise Offering Circular be filed with the state and may have additional requirements for a franchise to be sold in that state. These fifteen states are normally referred to as *Registration States*.

If a franchisor is going to sell franchises in a registration state, they must meet the individual requirements of that state. The fifteen states are: California, Hawaii, Illinois, Indiana, Maryland, Michigan, Minnesota, New York, North Dakota, Oregon, Rhode Island, South Dakota, Virginia, Washington, and Wisconsin.

Any state may have additional specific legislation regulating franchising. Individual states may also have exemptions for the first franchises sold in the state, or for *wealthy* or *sophisticated* franchisees. This legislation and exemptions will vary with every state. Check with your specific state. Most franchisors will also be familiar with the legislation affecting franchising in the individual states.

Chapter 29: Franchise History and Success

I have heard people say franchising is new. Franchising may be expanding rapidly in this country, but it is certainly not new. Franchising probably dates back to 2000 BC.

The story is that a farmer in China grew a product, which had such strong demand that he couldn't meet the demand. He then sold seeds with instructions for growing, processing, and marketing to other farmers for an initial fee and some percentage of future sales of the product.

Franchising has played some part in almost every major global economy since that time. Franchising played an important part of both the Greek and Roman empires.

◆ ◆ ◆

Franchising started to become a major factor in the United States around 1900. The first major franchises were called *Product Franchises* or *Product Distribution Franchises*. Automobile manufacturers, oil companies, and tire manufacturers were some of the companies awarding these product franchises.

These product franchises established franchisees that were referred to as dealers. These dealers sold the products under a common name and logo. These product franchises gave a dealer the right to sell the trademarked product. They also gave the dealer the right to use the name and logo.

The product franchise provided the dealer very little training or support except for product training and product warranty. No business system was provided. The dealer sometimes paid an initial franchise fee, but paid no royalty or ongoing franchise fee except for the margin paid on the product. Today, these same product franchisors offer complete business systems and ongoing support.

◆ ◆ ◆

Business System Franchises started in the late 1920's. Maid-Rite was probably one of the first, and started in Muscatine, Iowa. A Maid-Rite sandwich is a loose meat sandwich made from ground beef. A Maid-Rite sandwich has a specific recipe and is cooked in a specially designed cooker.

Around 1926 the founder of Maid-Rite started selling franchises. He provided the recipe and instructions for making a Maid-Rite sandwich. Originally, he provided instructions for making the special cooker and later provided the cooker.

It's my understanding that the original franchise fee was $50 plus an annual royalty fee of $25. There were no written contracts or agreements. Everything happened on a handshake.

I normally say no product is unique enough or good enough for the franchise to survive without a good business system. Maid-Rite may be the exception. The Maid-Rite franchise continued for three generations as a family owned business. It then had several very questionable owners.

As a franchisor, Maid-Rite did just about everything wrong, and made about every mistake possible, but survived. Maid-Rite is still around, partially because of their unique loose ground beef sandwich. Maid-Rite franchisees are primarily located in the Midwest.

The loose meat sandwich did get national publicity on the Roseanne TV show. Roseanne's husband at the time, Tom Arnold, came from Ottumwa, Iowa and loved the loose meat sandwiches.

Maid-Rite is again under new management. I wish them continued expansion and success. I love Maid-Rites.

◆　◆　◆

Franchising has done very well in the United States. It has made significant inroads in many industries. Almost any traditional *Mom* & *Pop* business you can think of now has competition from franchises. Franchise and chain operations take a larger and larger portion of the business as the small independent businesses close the doors.

A typical franchise operation will normally command a larger market share than its independent competitor. I've seen studies that in some industries, franchise operations will do two or three times the sales volume of their independent competitors. One study said franchises only accounted for 8% of all retail outlets, but accounted for 44% of all retail sales.

It's no wonder why the small mom and pop businesses continue to disappear. This change in business is sad in a way, but it's a fact of life. Don't make the mistake of thinking you can be the exception. It's unlikely you can make a business a success just because you're running it. You have to be able to market successfully and compete.

As I mentioned, I once sold real estate conversion franchises. When I went into a town where all the real estate firms were independents, they were able to compete on a level playing field.

As soon as one firm joined a franchise, that firm usually had an advantage in the market. This forced other firms to join a franchise in order to compete. If I visited these towns today, it would be safe to assume most of the leading firms will belong to a franchise. This is normally the case, but there will always be an exceptional independent firm that is a market leader.

◆　◆　◆

The International Franchise Association's Educational Foundation commissioned the National Economic Consulting Practice of Pricewaterhouse-Coopers to conduct a study on the "Economic Impact of Franchised Businesses." This study, completed in 2004 and based on 2001 economic data, showed 760,000 franchised establishments creating jobs for more than 18 million Americans and contributing $1.53 trillion to the U.S. economy.

The International Franchise Association's Educational Foundation also commissioned a study conducted by FRANdata Corp. called "Profile of Franchising 2007." This report stated more than 300 small business concepts had adapted the business-format model of franchising in 2006. The report goes on to say; there are now over 3,000 established business brands, which span 230 different lines of business.

Franchising is big business, and an integral part of

our economy. In my opinion, franchising is the most successful distribution system in the history of this country. Is a franchise opportunity right for you?

Chapter 30: Five levels of franchising

There are basically five levels of franchising. They are:

1. Franchisor

2. Regional Franchisor

3. Area Developer or Regional Developer

4. Multiple Unit Franchisee

5. Single Point Franchisee

The term *Master Franchisor* is sometimes used to describe what I will refer to as the *Franchisor* and sometimes used for what I will refer to as a *Regional Franchisor*. I will not use the term *Master Franchisor* in order to eliminate confusion. Be careful that you understand what someone is referring to when they use the term *Master Franchisor*.

◆ ◆ ◆

Let's first take a look at the *Franchisor*. An individual or company develops an original business concept and business system. The business concept and business system is very successful. It may have been duplicated successfully in several locations.

The decision is made to franchise the concept and business system. This individual or company is the franchisor. This could be the founder or someone that bought the rights to the business. Ray Kroc didn't start the original McDonalds, but he did franchise the business, and his company was the *Franchisor*.

Franchising is a complex and costly process. First, the concept must be proven successful, which is normally done by operating multiple locations successfully. Each location should be run independently using the business system and keeping separate books.

The business system must be written down in the form of manuals so future franchisees can implement the business system successfully. A training program must be developed for training new franchisees. A support system must be developed for supporting franchisees.

The Uniform Franchise Offering Circular must be completed. Individual filings must be done with any registration states in which franchises will be offered.

The names, trademarks, and logos must all be registered and protected. There may even be equipment that must be patented.

The franchisor must decide how to market their franchise. They must decide if they're going to award regional franchises, or if they're going to maintain complete control of all franchise development. Offering regional franchises usually allows faster growth with less capital, but some control is lost.

The franchising process is expensive and time consuming. It requires large amounts of capital. It is normally many years before the franchisor realizes a profit from franchising.

◆　◆　◆

A *Regional Franchisor* is someone who buys the rights to market and support franchises in a specific geographic area. The franchisor sells the region to the regional franchisor for an initial franchise fee.

The geographic area could be as small as a single town or television designated market area. It may be a state or several states. It might be as large as a country or continent in the case of international expansion.

The regional franchisor will be responsible for marketing the franchise in the region. The regional franchisor will also be responsible for some or all of the training and support of the franchisees in the region.

The regional franchisor is sometimes required to start and operate a prototype operation. This prototype operation can then be used to promote and market the franchise in the region. The prototype operation may also be used as a training facility for new franchisees in the region. The regional franchisor may also own and operate additional operations.

The regional franchisor will share in the initial franchise fee and any continuing royalty or franchise fees paid by the franchisees in the region. If the initial franchise fee is $40,000, the franchisor and the regional franchisor might share the fee 50-50 or $20,000 each.

The same would be true with any royalty or ongoing franchise fee. If the ongoing fee is 6% of sales, the franchisor and the regional franchisor might get 3% each.

The return on investment for regional franchisors can be very good once the region is fully developed.

The key is that the regional franchisor must market the franchise, find good franchisees, train his franchisees, support his franchisees, and develop the region.

Historically, the return and success rate for regional franchisors is higher than almost any other type of investment. Obviously, there can be no guarantees for the future or for any specific franchise.

◆ ◆ ◆

An *Area Developer* is sometimes called a *Regional Developer*. An area developer is an individual or company that commits to build and run all the franchise operations in a predetermined area. This area could be a single town or an entire state. An area developer does not sell franchises, as is the case with a regional franchisor.

This is one of the more expensive franchise options, as the area developer must have the resources necessary to fund all the locations he has committed to open. The area developer may be an investment group in some cases due to the size of the investment.

There will be some time schedule for opening the individual franchise operations. The number of locations and the approximate location of each will be predetermined in the Area Development Agreement.

This is an expensive franchise option, but is one way an individual can control the franchises in a given area. It also can be quite lucrative financially.

◆ ◆ ◆

The *Multiple Unit Franchisee* is the next level we'll discuss. Most franchisors offer an individual the option of owning more than one franchise location. Many franchisees do in fact own multiple franchise locations. This gives the franchisee greater income.

Some franchisors require a franchisee to commit to multiple locations initially. Some franchisors will award either a single franchise or multiples initially. Still other franchisors will only award a single franchise initially. The difference is dependent on the business model for the specific franchise and the role the franchisee will have in the operation of the business.

◆ ◆ ◆

Let's take a look at franchisors that only award multiple franchises. These franchisors may require a minimum commitment of three to five franchises.

The reasoning for this is usually twofold. They may want only more sophisticated investors with deep pockets and financial reserves. Another possible reason is that they do not want the owner involved in the day-to-day operation of the business.

These franchisors feel they have a very well defined and successful business system. They do not want the franchise owner involved in the day-to-day operations and possibly mess with the system. This may sound funny, but some franchisors have learned from experience.

◆ ◆ ◆

Many franchisors give a new franchisee the option to buy one, three, five, six or ten franchises initially. These are normally referred to as a three-pack, five-pack, six-pack or ten-pack.

The initial franchise fee is usually discounted when purchasing more than one franchise initially. The franchisee will be required to pay the franchise fee for all locations when the agreement is signed.

This option is one way a franchisee can control a bigger portion of a specific market from the beginning. There's always some predetermined schedule that the franchisee is to open each franchise point.

◆   ◆   ◆

Many franchisors will only award one franchise to an individual when they want that individual active in the day-to-day operation of the business. They may award the franchisee a second franchise, but only after the first operation is running successfully.

I had a client interested in a specific franchise in Charleston, South Carolina. Charleston was a two-point town for this specific franchise. My client wanted to buy both points. The franchisor wouldn't award more than one franchise initially.

The franchisor said they would love to have my client own both points in Charleston, but he had to get one up and running before awarding him the second point.

This made my client very unhappy, as he wanted to buy both points initially. I suggested that the franchisor might be looking out for his best interests. They obviously weren't just trying to sell franchises.

My client was awarded the single-point franchise. He was successful, and received the second point in a year or two. The franchisor knew what they were doing. Charleston is now one of the better operations in the system.

Chapter 31: Franchise Pros and Cons

The biggest negative normally perceived with buying a franchise is the perceived cost. In the Business Myths chapter we already discussed the commonly held belief that you shouldn't have to pay someone for something you can do yourself.

The initial franchise fee is what you pay for a proven business system. It may in fact be cheaper to pay the franchise fee than to develop a business system yourself. You may have to hire outside help at a cost in excess of the cost of the initial franchise fee. Just don't make the mistake of starting a business without a well thought out and detailed business system. I don't mean just some business plan with some financial projections.

I've had many clients ask what they get for the initial franchise fee. You may or may not get any tangible assets for that fee. You'll get the right to use the name and logo. This will have varying value depending on how well established the franchise is in your area. You'll probably get training, but you may have to pay your own travel and expenses for the training.

Some people have the perception that the franchisor is getting rich off that initial franchise fee. The fact is, most franchisors don't make any money from a new franchisee for about two years. Franchising a business concept is expensive. This is why some franchisors choose to sell regions. The regional franchisor can then share in the cost of adding new franchisees and growing.

◆ ◆ ◆

One advantage of a franchise is that they probably won't award you a franchise if you are under-capitalized. They won't let you try to "start small and grow." They know what the consumer expects and demands, and will make you start at that level.

The franchisor should have some idea of what you need for working capital and how many months of living expenses you should have in reserve. The franchisor may not be able to legally answer all these questions as they might be interpreted as earnings claims, but you can get the answers from other franchisees during validation.

If you don't have the recommended net worth and liquid assets required by the franchisor, don't even think about trying to do the same business on your own. Trying to start a business as an undercapitalized independent pretty much guarantees failure. Don't even think about it.

The biggest advantage of a franchise in my opinion is that the franchisee gets a proven business system and doesn't have to develop a system by trial and error. Trial and error can be very expensive.

Sometimes I think the interaction of franchisees is as important as the support the franchisor provides. The franchisor may help find a site for your business. They will probably require the site be approved. They know what you need.

The franchisor will probably recommend a design.

In some cases the franchisor may even handle the build-out. Again, they've learned which plans and designs work best.

A franchisee gets initial training. This is very important for a successful start-up. Training quality varies. Some franchises may even offer training for your employees. Check out what you get with the franchise.

A franchisee gets ongoing support. Again, the quality of this support varies from franchise to franchise. Some franchises go as far as hiring, training, and firing employees for the franchisee.

The franchisor will make recommendations for what products and services you offer. The franchisor will also make recommendations for how you price your products or services based on their experience. No trial and error.

The franchisor may offer bulk buying for your products and supplies. This can be a great help initially. You may later buy more locally, but certain standards will be required. It's hard to beat the price the franchisor will offer in most cases.

A part of any good franchise business system is marketing. You don't have to develop a marketing plan. It's done for you in most cases. Many franchises have advertising fees. These fees from all franchisees in a defined geographic area are then combined and used to purchase advertising. For example, if television advertising were a preferred media for a franchise, television markets would define the advertising areas. These television markets are normally defined as Designated Market Areas or DMAs.

Many people buying a franchise first think of the value of a recognizable name, logo, and image. Personally, I think the business system, training, and support are more important. Following the system and maintaining the required quality controls should put you on the path to success.

♦ ♦ ♦

One possible con of buying a franchise with a proven business system is that you must follow that system. You don't have the option of operating the business the way you want. This lack of individuality may be a blessing in the long run and save you money, but you must accept and follow the system.

Most studies show that the chance of failure with a franchise is about one tenth that of an independent business, but the fact that you buy a franchise in no way guarantees the business will be a success. Specific reasons for why a franchisee fails vary, but divorce is still a major reason. One general reason is that the franchisee did not follow the system. This is the danger of buying a franchise and then not following the system. In rare cases, the franchisor may revoke the franchise for extreme franchise agreement violations.

♦ ♦ ♦

It would be nice if you could get involved with a franchise that's well established with a good track record and a recognizable image. It would then be easy to validate the franchise.

The negative of a well-established franchise is, there are a limited number of franchises available, and all the franchises in your area may already be awarded. If you get involved with a franchise early, the name and image may not be established yet, but more locations are available for you to pick from.

There's really no good solution to this. Just find the business model that fits you and your goals.

If you're thinking of a regional franchisor opportunity or an area development opportunity, you must get involved with the franchise in the early stages of development. This is a situation where the saying of "getting in on the ground floor" is valid.

❖ ❖ ❖

I said the business system is the most important thing you got with a franchise. Don't get hung up on the product or service. A better hamburger, a better donut, a better ice cream, a better pizza sauce, or a better cup of coffee won't make you successful. Most of these things are a matter of personal taste and no guarantee of success.

Tastes vary. I like a good cup of Folgers Classic Roast coffee with caffeine and a little Half & Half. In fact, I like about twelve cups a day. One of my sons likes Starbuck's, and I don't have a clue what he orders. My point is that many things are a matter of personal taste. Your personal taste will not make you successful. A better business system will.

❖ ❖ ❖

We spent an entire chapter on market research. Market research is involved and can be more expensive than an individual can afford. One advantage of an established franchise is that most of the market research may be done for you. They'll know what defines a market for that franchise.

A Franchisor will know what geographic market is

needed for a successful franchise. This may be "X" population. It may be "X" population in "Y" miles. It may be "X" homes, or "X" homes in "Y" miles. It may be "X" homes with an income over "Z." It may be "X" number of businesses or "X" businesses in "Y" miles.

The franchisor should know what size market is needed for success. It makes no sense to give a franchisee too small a market, as the franchisor's success is dependent on the franchisee's success.

If your franchise is a fixed location type, your agreement might say that no other franchises may be awarded within "X" miles. Your agreement may say they will only award "X" franchises in a defined market.

If your franchise is not a fixed location type, your franchise agreement may list the county(s), town(s), or zip code(s) that define your market. The franchisor normally awards a larger market than is needed for an individual franchisee. I know of some franchises where the franchisee goes to the customer, and the awarded area is so large that the franchisor recommends only marketing to one fourth of the area initially.

Some franchisors restrict doing business outside your defined market area. The franchisor can control where you physically locate a business, but they can't legally control where you do business.

For example, I've seen agreements that define a specific geographic area for the awarded franchise. They then list penalties for doing business outside the defined area. The first offense might be a warning. The second offense could be a fine. Repeated offenses would be listed as grounds for revoking the franchise agreement.

These restrictions are not enforceable as our federal government considers them a restraint of trade. I do recommend following the franchisor's recommendations anyway as it's in the best interests of maintaining good working relationships with your franchisor and neighboring franchisees.

Ongoing market research is another advantage of a franchise. A successful franchise with a large number of franchisees will have feedback from all those franchisees. The franchisor will know what's happening in the marketplace.

The combined strength of all the franchisees serve as a market research firm that most independent businesses could never afford. Successful franchises evolve as the market changes.

Look at McDonalds. McDonalds started with hamburgers, cheeseburgers, fries, and shakes. Most of today's menu came from the franchisees, not the franchisor.

McDonalds didn't offer breakfast for many years. When McDonalds did start offering breakfast, some franchisees were so opposed to the idea that they sold their franchises. Think about the money McDonald's makes from breakfast today. Markets change.

◆ ◆ ◆

The synergy of having other franchises in your market will improve your image and make you money. One of my clients was awarded the franchises for three locations in his market. The market had been scheduled for six locations.

The same day my client signed the franchise

agreements; he commented that he hoped the other three locations would be awarded soon. My client understood that when the market had six stores open, each store would make more money than with only one store, or three stores in the market.

Some people don't understand synergism. They think they can open one store and get all the business in the market. If this were true, they could make more money. Unfortunately, it doesn't work that way. If you're one of these people who doesn't understand how synergism works, you probably don't want a franchise.

◆　◆　◆

A franchisor's growth and success is totally dependent on the success of its franchisees. No franchise can be successful in the long run without successful franchisees. The relationship between a franchisor and the franchisees is truly an interdependent relationship.

For this reason, a franchisor is more particular about whom they award a franchise. Some people have the impression a franchisor will sell a franchise to anyone who will write a check for the initial franchise fee. You may not be able to buy a franchise. Yes, there is a franchise fee you will pay, but you still have to be approved by the franchisor and be awarded the franchise.

Some people mistakenly think this is a rubber stamp. Not true. The franchisor knows that a bad franchisee is more trouble than they are worth.

I know of one franchisor that invites prospective franchisees for a review at the corporate headquarters when they're ready to buy. The prospective franchisee is expected to come with a check and be ready to sign an agreement if approved.

It's almost like a job interview. The franchisor's top staff interviews the prospect and votes yes or no for awarding the franchise.

Is the process a rubber stamp? Not quite. The last I heard, four out of ten prospects for this franchise were sent home with their check and no franchise.

◆　◆　◆

As a franchisee you'll have rules and restrictions on how you operate your business. Most of these are for your own good. If you have a problem with this, a franchise may not be for you.

I've had many clients say the franchise agreement is one-sided, and they're absolutely right. The franchisor must maintain control of the franchise in order to maintain the image of the franchise. I normally tell clients to look at the franchise agreement as a way of protecting them and their image after they are a franchisee.

I often use the example of the franchise agreement protecting a franchisee from a neighboring franchisee doing something that would hurt their reputation. If you owned a McDonalds, you'd try to maintain a certain image. If a neighboring McDonalds franchisee puts in lap dancing during a slow time in the afternoon, it probably wouldn't do much for your image. The franchise agreement would protect you from having this happen.

The franchise agreement is a legal contract and I would recommend having an attorney review it, but please use an attorney who's familiar with franchising.

An attorney who's familiar with franchising will know that most things in the agreement are not negotiable due to the Uniform Franchise Offering Circular filing requirements.

I've seen attorneys waste their client's money by spending hours *red lining* things they would like to change on the agreement. An attorney familiar with franchising would know better.

◆   ◆   ◆

From my perspective as a business consultant, franchising offers many options to fit an individual's talents, resources, and goals. Franchising offers opportunities for the individual who just wants to create a job, as well as the individual who wants to build an empire.

There are franchise opportunities that require the owner be active in the daily operations of the business. There are franchises that require multiple operations so the owner is strictly managing the operations and not involved in the day-to-day operations. There are even franchises that are strictly investment opportunities and don't want the owner involved in the business at all except for looking at monthly statements.

Franchise opportunities give a lot of options. It may be easier to find a fit with a franchise opportunity, but franchise opportunities are not for everyone. Again, the key is to ignore the product or service and look at the business model.

Chapter 32: Make the Decision to Gather Data

Your first step, after reading this book, is to make a decision to gather data. Up to this point, most of your decisions may have been made on perceptions and emotions. Now it's time to do the research and get the facts.

Don't make a decision to go into business, or make an investment in a business yet. This is still a premature decision. The next step is to make a decision to investigate if self-employment or a business investment is right for you. It may not be right for you, or it may not be right for you at this time.

I've had clients investigate self-employment options and decide self-employment is not right for them. This is great. At least they know and they can now be happy in their job.

I have clients who decide a business investment isn't right for them. That's great. Now they can be more comfortable with where they're presently investing.

I have clients who investigate self-employment and determine the timing isn't right for some reason. Maybe they need to get their finances in order and accumulate more liquid capital. They now have a better understanding of what's involved and can make an informed decision.

Self-employment may be a good option for someone, but just not at this time. I've had several clients call me years later and say, "We're ready now."

These clients now own their own business and are on their way to reaching their goals.

You'll notice I said, "We." If you have a spouse or significant other in your life, they *must* be involved at this point in your investigation. This is very important. The first step for your spouse or significant other is to read this book.

If the spouse or significant other isn't involved at this point, they'll be resistant to what you've learned when you spring it on them. This is just human nature. If they're not involved from the beginning, they'll be more resistant to any change.

I've had people of both sexes want to do the preliminary investigation on their own. After they think self-employment might be a good option, they tell their spouse. This is a big mistake. Their spouse is now negative. A husband and wife must discover if self-employment is a good option together.

I made this mistake myself when starting Lee Motors, Inc, and buying the Ford-Mercury dealership. I sat at our kitchen table one day with one of my silent investors. My wife was in the room listening. She said, "You're serious about this aren't you?" I said, "Yes, the offer's already been accepted." It probably hurt our relationship. She should have been involved from the beginning.

I have had guys say that their wife goes along with whatever they decide. Wrong, this never seems to be the case. They're just kidding themselves with a decision this large. Even if the wife does go along, it won't help their relationship.

I had one client insist his wife went along with

whatever he decided. He was ready to sign a franchise agreement when he surprised his wife with the idea. He's still in his job today. He can't get his wife to even consider the option now.

Wives may have blindly gone along with their husband's decisions in *the good old days*, but those days are gone, and thank goodness. I think it is a lot better to have a partner.

◆ ◆ ◆

Stan, an older cousin of mine, moved back home to a small town in Iowa from California in the 50s. He had a family with five sons and no job. Everyone thought he'd gone crazy, but Stan had something going for him. He could sell. He went into business selling stainless steel pots and pans.

Stan sold his pots and pans at parties. He'd have someone book a dinner party and invite their friends and neighbors. Stan would always arrive late. He wanted to make sure everyone else had arrived. He would then cook dinner while explaining the value of his product. He made it look easy and fun.

After everyone had a delicious dinner, he'd take one couple at a time into another room to close the sale. He'd obviously start with the couples that had given him the strongest buying signals.

Now I get to the reason I'm giving you this story. If a man or woman came to the party without their spouse, Stan wouldn't talk to them or sell them a set of pots and pans. Stan knew this might alienate the spouse and kill any chance of a sale. If the attending spouse wanted to buy, Stan simply told them they'd have to attend another dinner party with their spouse.

Don't kid yourself. Your spouse or significant other must be involved from the beginning.

◆ ◆ ◆

The decision to investigate self-employment should be made long before making a decision to be self-employed. I've had clients quit their jobs so they could devote all their attention to finding and starting a business. This is a huge mistake. I never recommend this. If you have the option, I recommend staying in your job as long as you can.

Monthly expenses for you and your family continue whether you have a job or not. Money needed to live while you look for the right opportunity depletes your investment capital. The only exception is if you're independently wealthy. Unfortunately, most of us aren't independently wealthy.

Having no income puts additional pressure on an individual to find a business and make a decision quickly. The spouse may also put more pressure on an individual in this situation. This added pressure pushes the individual to make premature decisions.

Chapter 33: When to Start

When should you start investigating self-employment or business investment opportunities? The answer is easy. Now is the time. Don't fall into the trap of *getting ready to get ready*. This is pure procrastination.

If you're starting your investigation while you're still in your job, you'll have to designate so many hours per day, or per week, to investigate if self-employment or a business investment is right for you.

Getting ready to get ready is a great excuse. I've had clients who said they had to get this or that done before they could start their investigation. This is a classic excuse, and in most cases a safe way of avoiding investigating if self-employment is the right option.

Why would someone want to avoid making a commitment to investigate options? One major subconscious reason is the fear of actually finding a great option that will give them the vehicle to achieve their goals. They would then be forced to *put up or shut up*. This can be very scary.

◆   ◆   ◆

You may think there's a possibility you'll be laid off in the future. Maybe your company is involved in a merger and you don't know if your job is stable. Don't wait for the hammer to fall. Start investigating options now.

You may or not find a self-employment option that fits your goals. You may or may not get laid off. You may or may not find another job immediately. You can't control getting laid off. You can't control getting another job. You *can* control investigating your options. One of the toughest decisions you may face is finding a self-employment opportunity that fits your goals, and you don't get laid off. Personally, I don't think that's such a bad problem.

I had a client in Tulsa who always wanted his own business, but was always afraid to make the step. Due to a merger, he expected to be laid off. We found a business that fit his talents, resources, and goals. He kept the franchisor he'd selected informed, but didn't sign the final franchise agreement until his employer gave him notice. The week after they let him go with his severance pay, he attended training for his new franchise business.

Another classic excuse is timing. "The economy is bad, and I have to wait until this recession is over." This is just an excuse. I've heard that more millionaires are normally made in times of recession than in times of inflation. I'm not sure that's true, but I guess there are always opportunities for people that look for them.

There are businesses that thrive in a recession. There are businesses that are unaffected by economic conditions. One franchise I've worked with has shown consistent sales increases of over 40% in bad economic times. So why are you waiting?

You may find a business model that's right for you that does better in good economic times. Great. Now you're in a position to time your start-up for when the economy recovers.

You need to start your business and get all the bugs worked out. You want to be running smoothly when the economy recovers. If you wait for the economy to recover before starting to look for a business, you may be too late to take full advantage of the economic recovery. The saying "A day late and a dollar short" doesn't refer to luck.

◆　◆　◆

The market share your company has is directly related to profits in most cases. My experience is that most businesses increase their market share during a time of recession. The best most businesses can do in a boom market is maintaining their market share.

This makes sense if you think about it. It's kind of like nature and the survival of the fittest. In a down market, a few competitors always close. When a competitor closes, their customers are picked up by the remaining competition, thus increasing their market share.

When the market turns, a business retains the new customers, the increased market share, and increased profits. Starting your business in a down market is not a bad thing, if you're properly financed.

◆　◆　◆

I mentioned ordering a large inventory when I first took over the Ford-Mercury dealership. We sold those cars. We had no choice but to sell the cars. The large inventory resulted in the highest volume month that year. This didn't surprise me. What did surprise me is when I looked back at the year, that high volume month was also our second highest average gross per vehicle for the year. I would have expected a low gross. We had inventory. We had a good selection of product. We had an opportunity and took advantage of it.

When I looked back on a five-year history in the car dealership, I discovered something else interesting. The economy didn't make a lot of difference on our bottom line. The only thing that seemed to make a difference was how smart I worked personally.

The gas shortages of 1973 may have been real or manipulated. It doesn't matter which, as the consumer perceived it as a real shortage, and in some areas of the country this proved accurate. The economy was hurting. A lot of car dealerships closed, but Lee Motors, Inc. had one of its better years.

Lee Iacocca, the president of Ford at the time, said, "The American car buyer wants economy, and will pay any price to get it." This sounds like a contradiction until you stop and think about it. Car buyers were looking for economy, but didn't want to give up the luxury and convenience features they were used to having.

Prior to that time, small economy cars were generally sold with very few options. That all started to change in 1973. Change creates opportunity if we look for it.

We were a relatively small dealership, and that put us in a position to change our inventory quickly. I had a competing Pontiac-Buick dealer that had a huge used car inventory of large, heavy, gas eating luxury cars. The gas crunch almost broke him. The value of that used car inventory dropped and he couldn't retail or wholesale those cars.

I had a couple come in with a new Chevrolet Monte Carlo loaded with optional equipment. They only had a few thousand miles on the car. Because of the gas shortage, the couple wanted to trade it in for a loaded Ford Pinto station wagon I had in stock.

I gave the couple a trade price, but told them I wouldn't make the deal that day. I asked them to go home and think about taking that kind of a loss on the Monte Carlo. They came back in a few days and made the deal.

Most sales managers would have been very upset with me for not closing the deal the first day. I could have lost the deal, but I didn't, and the couple remained loyal customers my entire time at the dealership.

◆　◆　◆

I'm not in any way saying ignore economic conditions. Actual conditions and conditions perceived by your customers are an important part of the market. Try to anticipate changes and react to the opportunities these changes create.

When it comes right down to it, there is no right time, except now. Don't make excuses. Make that decision now to start your investigation and gather data.

Deciding to go into business for yourself is premature at this time. You may discover that owning a business isn't right for you. You'll face that decision at some point in the future when you have more data and facts.

Chapter 34: Define Your Goals and Resources

If you're going to find a business that gets you to your goals, you must define your resources, talents, strengths, weaknesses, and goals. You must put them in writing. Start a list for each. This will take a lot more time and thought than you think. Don't kid yourself. Be honest.

The place to start is financial because it is finite. Develop a balance sheet for yourself. List all assets and liabilities. You'll need this later anyway. What's your net worth? What's your liquid capital?

You next need to look at your current cash flow. What are your income sources? What's your salary? Does your spouse or significant other have a salary? Will you quit your job? Will your spouse or significant other quit their job? Do you have other sources of income?

You next need to look at your current cash flow. What are your income requirements for your lifestyle? Can you cut back on your living expenses? What is the minimum amount you'll need to live?

If one salary continues that covers your minimum living expenses, it means you won't have a negative cash flow. If not, how much is the negative cash flow? This is the amount you'll need to add to your start-up costs. These are some very important parameters for looking at options.

The monthly amount you'll need to subsidize your

living expenses is the key number now. You'll need to have this financial reserve to live on until your business can support you. How long will that be? An old rule of thumb is that a new business would take two years to make money. Hopefully, your business will do better than that, but that will be part of the validation process that will be covered later in the book.

Again, be honest. Be realistic about how much you'll need to live on. Be conservative about how long the business will need to support you. Remember, undercapitalization is the number one cause of business failure.

◆ ◆ ◆

I once knew an individual in the franchise brokerage and consulting business who said, "Don't worry about the money. If you find the right option, the money will flow." I don't agree with this statement. It sounds too much like our government to me, and to the best of my knowledge, none of us can print money.

You do have other options for financing including family and friends. Another option is some sort of creative financing like we talked about.

I have had clients say, "The investment depends on the opportunity." This statement is just plain bull. Don't kid yourself. Be honest. The people you'll be working with will recognize this statement as BS, and you'll lose credibility.

◆ ◆ ◆

The next step is to look at your other resources. What are your talents? What are your strengths and your weaknesses? What are your spouse's talents, strengths, and weaknesses? No partnerships, except for spouses and significant others, please. You already know how I feel about partnerships.

After writing down your talents, strengths, and weaknesses, go over the list, marking what you like and dislike doing. Write down what role you want in the business. Doing what you like on a daily basis will help ensure your happiness in your new business.

I believe Gallup did a survey of a relatively small sample of franchisees. This survey showed that 92% of the franchisees surveyed were happy with the financial return on investment, but only 65% of the franchisees surveyed would make the same investment again.

I think this clearly shows that there is more to meeting an individual's goals than just the financial return. Make sure you'll be happy with your daily role in the business.

◆　◆　◆

You can either sell or you can't. You're either happy when you're in a sales mode or you aren't. This does not depend on the product or service you are selling.

I've had clients say they could sell if they believe in the product or service. This statement is a cop out. We're not talking about you being a grifter in a con. We're talking about if you can sell. I've seen people who can't sell, try to sell something they strongly believe in. They get extremely upset and unhappy with any rejection they get. It just doesn't work. Don't kid yourself.

Either you're a good manager of people, or you aren't. Either you like to manage people, or you don't.

This answer is basically the same for managing a few employees or a large number of employees. The answer is basically the same if you are managing professionals or minimum wage employees. The basics don't change. Again, don't kid yourself.

You have other talents and weaknesses you'll be able to identify. Write them down, think about them, and revise your list of strengths and weaknesses.

If you have a spouse or someone who knows you well, have him or her review the list and make comments. This is a great way to get your spouse or significant other involved in the process.

If your spouse or significant other is going to be involved in the business, you both need to write down your strengths and weaknesses. You both need to review the other's list.

◆ ◆ ◆

When I look at myself, I like to think I have some strengths. I consider myself an honest person. I have a good work ethic. I can sell. I am very analytical and organized. These are some of my strengths.

One of my weaknesses is that I am too trusting. I tend to believe people, and take them at their word. This is a weakness to the point of being naïve sometimes. This weakness has caused many of the mistakes and problems in my life.

Be honest. It may hurt. You may not even like to acknowledge your weaknesses. Now is the time. It'll be better than having your weaknesses bite you in the butt later.

◆ ◆ ◆

You probably have other people in your circle of

influence with special talents. They may be friends or relatives. This is a good time to identify them.

You may want to draw on their talents later, but not yet. You may need to compensate them, but sometimes they'll help you for free. Maybe they can benefit with business from you later.

Again, write them down. Check the lists with your spouse and revise.

◆　◆　◆

I had a client, whom we'll call Sam. Sam lived in Atlanta and was a very successful sales manager in the telecom industry. He was successful, but unhappy with his job, and found it very frustrating. He just wanted to sell.

I had another client we'll call Linn. Linn sold fraternal life insurance in the Midwest. Her work ethic and sheer tenacity made her successful. In spite of Linn's financial success she was very unhappy in her job.

Both Sam and Linn were able to find self-employment options where their role in the business fit their individual personalities. You can too. We'll talk more about Sam and Linn in a later chapter

◆　◆　◆

The next step is to write down your goals. Yes, I know you want to get rich. Most people would like to get rich, but would never pay the price to achieve that goal.

Some people are exceptions and are empire builders. These are rare individuals and getting rich has little to do with it. It is the challenge that motivates them and makes them happy. The money is just a way of keeping score.

I knew an individual who took his company public. His company then merged with a competitor. He retired, but was bored. He became a client and started the process I'm describing.

He listed one of his goals as finding a little business to give him something to do in his retirement. Once in the validation, he discovered he didn't really want a small business. He wanted to build another empire. That's who he was and what he did. He found a regional franchise opportunity that fit his talents, resources, and goals. He's building another empire. Making money had very little to do with it.

What are your goals? Let's forget getting rich unless you're that rare empire builder, but maybe you just want to make more money. Maybe you want to work fewer hours, or have more flexibility in those hours. Maybe you travel and want to get off the road. Maybe you want to spend more time with your family.

Maybe you're unhappy in your present job. Maybe they want you to move. Where do you want to live?

Maybe you want more or less contact with your customers. Maybe you want to manage more or fewer people. Maybe you want to sell or don't want to sell.

Maybe you just want to create a secure job for yourself. Maybe you want to build an empire. May be you're just looking for an investment. Maybe you want to be an absentee owner and have minimal contact with the daily operations of the business.

Maybe you just want to control your own destiny. Everyone is different. This will take a lot of thought and will be revised many times. Be as honest with yourself as you can.

◆　◆　◆

One possible goal is investing in a business for retirement. This goal is probably to provide some retirement income. You may want to start the business before retiring from your present career or you may want to wait until after retiring.

Maybe you've retired and are bored. Maybe golf and fishing aren't enough for you. Marla says I don't, "idle well". I have to stay busy.

You may or may not want to be active in the business. The goal may be a business you can work either full or part-time after retiring from your present career.

The February 2007 AARP Bulletin stated that 7.4 million baby boomers are self-employed, that only 44% of new businesses last four years. The AARP Bulletin asked the question, "Is launching a start-up late in life risky?"

There are very few guarantees in life. The object of this process is to reduce that risk.

◆　◆　◆

I mentioned having your spouse involved from the beginning. When it comes to defining goals, you both must write your own list. Then compare and revise. This is an essential step in the total process.

Chapter 35: Research Resources

How and where do you find a business to investigate? Some of the first places that come to mind are:

1. Internet

2. Newspaper classified ads

3. Magazines

4. Trade publications

5. Networking

6. Brokers

7. Government agencies

8. Consultants

All of these are good sources and there are many more. The possibilities are almost unlimited.

◆ ◆ ◆

The Internet offers almost unlimited options. You can get lost in the Internet. You can invest huge amounts of time searching, and unfortunately most of it will be confusing and unproductive. The question is what to use for an initial screening.

Classified ads are a good source because they'll be advertising in a specific area. Businesses offered for sale privately and listed by a business broker may be advertised. Business opportunities may be advertised.

Franchise resales may be advertised in local papers.

Magazines and trade publications will be more focused. Trade publications will be focused on specific industries. Magazines like "Entrepreneur" will focus on new franchise and business opportunities.

Networking can be an effective business investigation source. Talk to business owners or people who have been business owners. Don't bother talking to people who have never been in business. You don't need their perceptions that are probably inaccurate.

Business and franchise brokers can be a good source. They can help you focus. Just remember a broker gets paid when they make a sale. They're interested in making a commission, and not necessarily in helping you meet your goals. They're likely to direct you to opportunities where they make the largest commission.

◆ ◆ ◆

There are a variety of government agencies you can use. The advantage of these is they're normally free or available for a minimal charge. The disadvantage is that the help they offer is normally limited, and in my opinion most don't address the most critical issues like market research, marketing, and most importantly whether or not the business fits your goals.

The Small Business Administration (SBA) can be of help in obtaining financing. We discussed the SBA in the chapter on financing. I haven't found the SBA to be much help in other areas of business start-up. The good thing is that any help the SBA can give you is free.

SCORE is an acronym for Service Corps of Retired Executives. I think the level of help available from SCORE will vary from area to area. They're normally good at helping set up accounting, payroll, and tax systems. My experience is that they're weak in other areas. The good thing about SCORE is that any help they can give is free.

Most community colleges will offer courses in entrepreneurship or starting a business. Enrollment fees are low. The course will probably touch on many areas of business. The downside is that nothing is covered in-depth and is not specific to your needs.

Many states, counties, cities, and universities have economic development or small business development individuals or departments. The help these agencies and individuals can provide will vary. Names and titles will also vary. You'll have to track them down and contact them. The primary objective of these individuals is to create new jobs in their area, so the more jobs you create, the more help you can expect.

Retaining or using a business consultant, business coach or franchise broker may also be an excellent resource. We will talk more about this option in the next chapter.

Chapter 36: Investigation & Validation

By now you should have read this entire book to this point. If not, go back and read the sections you skipped. You can't skip steps in this process. I can hear some of you say, "I know what I want to do, and I don't want to waste time with things that aren't relevant to me." This attitude can be a huge mistake, because "You don't know what you don't know," and what you don't know can be the difference between success and failure.

◆　◆　◆

You're now ready to start. You've identified your goals, resources, and talents. You know the life you want to live. You know your strengths and weaknesses. You've identified your business knowledge and lack of knowledge. You know how much money you have to work with. You've also identified all this for your spouse or significant other, and he or she is totally involved with the investigation.

Remember, you haven't made a decision to go into business for yourself yet. You're investigating if self-employment and/or a business investment is a good option for you by looking at different opportunities.

We've discussed independent business startup, buying an existing business, business opportunities, and franchises. We now need to determine which you want to investigate. It's not unusual to start with one option, find it doesn't meet your needs and move to another option.

For example, someone will start out looking to buy an existing business and discover there just isn't anything that fits his or her goals, resources, and talents. At this point, they may move on to franchising.

As we've mentioned, there are over 5,500 franchises in over 80 industries in franchising alone. The options are almost too many to comprehend. Where do you start? How do you do your initial screening of opportunities?

Most people look at the product or service to make their initial screening. This is what I call an *Outside-In* approach. This approach means initial screening is done on your personal perception of the product or service. It has nothing to do with your role in the business.

Perception of a product or service is often based on emotion and personal taste. Your personal taste in coffee or pastries isn't enough to bet your future.

How many coffee shops have closed, taking their owner's savings down the drain, because the owner was confident they had a better blend of coffee? With the possible exception of Maid-Rite, I know of no product that's unique enough and good enough to carry a business without a good business system.

I know of one individual who started a pizza business with the unique twist of selling both pizza and ice cream. He was very successful and started franchising. He considered his pizza sauce the key to the success and felt the business system wasn't that important. As a result, he lost all his franchisees and had to start over with a solid business system.

No product or service will appeal to everyone. A person who loves to cook and bake from scratch may not see or recognize the need for pre-cooked foods. The saying "One size fits all" seldom works.

When Dodge came out with their current pickup design, market research showed half the sample surveyed loved the design and half the sample hated the design. The previous philosophy of pickup designers focused on a design that wasn't objectionable to anyone. The problem with that philosophy is that no one really loved the design either.

Dodge went with the controversial design and it did very well. Management recognized they could never please everyone. They would never put Chevrolet, Ford, and GMC out of the pickup business. Dodge did achieve a new design that enough people loved to increase their market share.

◆   ◆   ◆

Most people define their search based on three things. These three things are:

1. Prior experience

2. A perception of demand

3. Something they think will be fun.

Let's take a look at each. Prior experience in business is very good and essential if you're thinking about an independent start-up or even buying an existing business. Limiting your search to one industry may not give you the opportunity you need to reach your goals. You may also have a problem with a non-compete agreement. Maybe you're coming out of the corporate world where you've only been exposed to one aspect of an industry.

◆　◆　◆

A perception of demand is probably the most dangerous of all reasons people use to select a business. Just because you like pizza and there's not a convenient place to pick up a pizza on your way home from work isn't a good reason to open a pizza business close to your home. There may not be a lot of people who like pizza in your neighborhood. Maybe there're just not enough people in your neighborhood to support a pizza business.

I'm of Norwegian descent. I love good lefsa. I'm not naïve enough to think I could open a successful lefsa store. You may not even know what lefsa is. Lefsa is a Norwegian potato crepe. Why would you want to buy lefsa? My personal tastes aren't relevant in starting a business.

◆　◆　◆

The third natural thing is to look for something that sounds fun. I often hear the saying, "You have to love what you're doing." This is true, but the saying refers to your role in the business and not the product or service.

I mentioned *The E-Myth Revisited* by Michael Gerber earlier. The woman in the book loved to make pies, but she had to quit making pies in order to have her business survive. You may love pie, but if you start a business selling pies, you may not be making pies personally.

People often think they can turn a hobby into a

business. I had a client who told me he'd ruined one hobby by turning it into a business, and he wasn't going to ruin his other hobby by doing the same.

If you love to play golf, why would you want a business involving golf? You would now be working while others are out having fun playing golf. You still may be able to do what you like with your hobby as a business, but it may not be a profitable business. Being a pro golfer sounds fun, but since I have trouble playing bogey golf, I might not make much money.

I know a farmer who took up golf in his fifties. He converted land on his farm to a driving range. He also put in a chipping area and a putting green. He has a minor charge for the balls on the driving range. The chipping and putting are free.

He put up a building where he installed three computerized golf machines for winter golf. He also makes custom golf clubs, and gives golf lessons.

There is very little population in the area. He may spend more time maintaining the driving range than people do using the driving range. He may now have a very expensive hobby. I'd be surprised if the business ever does anything except provide him with a tax write-off.

There are a lot of *fun* businesses out there, if you only want a hobby. I often have clients ask about franchises with a product they love, or sounds fun. I usually just ask if they are looking for a fun hobby, or want to make money.

◆ ◆ ◆

The *Outside-In* approach looks at the product or service usually based on personal taste and emotion. I prefer the *Inside-Out* approach that ignores the product or service. This approach matches an individual to a business system and model, and ignores the product or service.

Professional help may be needed to implement the *Inside-Out* approach. A professional business consultant or business coach can't make decisions for you, but can help you get past your perceptions and emotions. A consultant cannot guarantee your success, but may be able to help you ask the right questions.

The consultant must be familiar with different business models and systems. Franchise knowledge is essential because of the many options available even if you're not initially interested in a franchise. You need to keep all options open at this point in your investigation.

The consultant may be compensated on a fee basis, or as a commissioned broker, or both. If you are paying the consultant strictly on an hourly basis, it can get expensive. If paid solely on commission, you need to feel comfortable he or she is working in your best interests and not just trying to make a sale. When I work with a client, I never consider the brokerage fee, but I've been told I am too honest. I have to admit I'm not normal in a lot of ways.

Select a consultant or coach you feel comfortable working with. If you decide to work with a consultant or coach, work with that individual exclusively. Keep him or her informed of anything and everything involving your investigation. Secrets are not in your best interest, and limit the help the consultant or coach can give you.

◆ ◆ ◆

I recommend several steps for your investigation and validation. I'm going to use an example of investigating franchises, as they offer the most options and require the most steps. Options other than franchising will still have the same sequence of steps, but maybe not as many.

I recommend looking at only one to three options at a time. Looking at more than three makes the investigation too shallow and decisions are made on perception instead of facts and data.

As a consultant, I've recommended from one to three options to investigate. I often start with only one option at a time. We can then learn what's right and what's wrong with that business model. With that new knowledge, I can then recommend another business model for my client to investigate.

When learning the business I would present three business models. I discovered three options were too much for the client in most cases, and they would only investigate two anyway. They usually dropped one based on emotion and perception, which is the last thing I wanted to achieve.

I sometimes ask my client to look at two business models in the beginning. When I do this, one option may be a franchise and the other may be a business opportunity. This can be very educational for my client.

I sometimes ask my client to investigate two options in franchising. One option may be a single point franchise business model, and the other may be a multiple or a regional franchise business model. Again, this can be very educational for my client.

If you're doing this investigation on your own, I still recommend never looking at more than two or three options at once. Try to look at different types of business models. If you have a spouse or significant other, he or she will be involved and can act as your coach.

Learn from the business models you validate and make new selections based on what you learn. Again, look at business models and systems, not the product and service. I cannot stress this enough.

◆ ◆ ◆

The normal thing to do when you start thinking about self-employment or a business investment is to talk to your friends and relatives about it. Don't! This is a huge mistake. All you'll get is their emotions and perceptions. This is worse than your own emotions and perceptions and this is exactly what we're trying to avoid.

◆ ◆ ◆

The next step is to develop a list of questions about the business system and the business model. The first thing everyone thinks of is "How much money can I make?" Yes, this is important, but irrelevant if the business model doesn't fit your talents and resources.

I can't give you a list of questions. You have to develop your own list, based on your goals and resources. Things like profit break-even, time to break-even, and return-on-investment are the obvious.

Questions about the business system are not so obvious. What is the marketing? What type of sales?

How many and what type of employees? Probably the most important question is what your role and/or your spouse's role in the business system will be. What will you have to do to be successful?

Don't make any assumptions about a business model. For example, you may think you know how a business markets its product or service. Don't assume you know. Ask questions to confirm how they do it.

Make an organized list of questions. Don't think you can just wing it. Have your spouse develop a list also. Then compare and combine. Your spouse will have different questions.

Keep a copy of these questions on your computer. Leave space between questions to write answers. Run copies so you'll be able to take notes as you ask questions. This list will evolve as you learn more about business models.

Again, I'm going to use a franchise model as it involves the most steps. The first step after selecting a model is to contact the franchisor. Someone from the franchise will get back to you. This will normally be someone in franchise sales or franchise development.

The initial contact from the franchisor will set a time for a longer meeting by phone. I recommend this be done at a time your spouse can participate, if possible. They may also mail you some material and probably refer you to their web site. You may have already seen the site, but now you need to study it before the next meeting.

The franchise will now ask you for information including financial information. You'll have already compiled this information. It's needed by the franchisor to qualify you. This is necessary to make sure you have the resources to be successful with the franchise. This is in your best interest. Don't be secretive. It serves no good purpose. The franchisor wants to be sure you're a viable candidate for their franchise before sharing proprietary information with you.

Read and study any information you receive from the franchisor before every contact with them. You'll need this information before the meeting or you'll be wasting your time. As you read, listen, and learn, you'll expand and revise your list of questions.

At some point, you'll receive a Uniform Franchise Offering Circular. We talked about what needs to be in this document. Sign and return the acknowledgement that you received the document. Signing the receipt obligates you to nothing, but is a necessary step.

I don't recommend going over this document in detail at this time. If you want to read it, fine, but I don't even encourage that. There's definitely no reason to waste time and money on an attorney yet.

There are two things in the document you do need initially. These two things are a listing of all the franchisees in the system, and any earnings claims the franchisor is making.

At some point you'll want to call franchisees from this list. The franchisor may give you specific franchisees to call, but you'll want to call others from the list. You may want to call them all.

The franchisor can't make any earnings claims of any kind other than those listed in the UFOC. Be careful to read any earnings claims, including every footnote.

Many franchises don't list any earnings claims in their UFOC. There can be many reasons for not showing any earnings claims and this shouldn't be construed as a negative for the franchise.

Remember, this isn't true with business opportunities that are not a franchise. They can tell you anything, including telling you everyone will be millionaires overnight.

Some other things that might be of interest are initial franchise fees, royalties, advertising funds, territories, and a copy of the actual franchise agreement. Most of this will be presented and covered verbally by the franchisor also.

◆　◆　◆

After you talk to the person from franchise development, the next step is to talk to other franchisees. You can ask the franchisor for recommendations. Obviously, the franchisor will give you the names of the most successful franchisees. You may ask for franchisees in your market area, or in similar markets to yours.

You may want to ask for franchisees who have similar backgrounds to yours. It's probably good to talk to new franchisees and some with an established history. You may want to talk to franchisees who are not doing well.

I once had a client who investigated a franchise. He went to visit one of the poorest performing franchisees in the system. I thought this might sour him on the franchise. It didn't. He commented, "If that idiot is making money, I'll do just fine."

◆　◆　◆

After you receive the UFOC with a listing of all the franchisees, you can talk to each and every one if you wish. When you talk to franchisees, respect their time. Remember, they're independent owners. They're not obligated to talk to you, but you'll normally find them very accommodating. Use the same list of questions you've already compiled.

One of the nice things about a franchise is the option of talking to other franchisees. This isn't an option when considering most other business options.

When talking to the franchisor, everything about the franchise will naturally be great. You may not get as shining a report from the franchisees. The franchisor is limited to giving only the earnings claims listed in the UFOC. This is not true with the franchisees. They're independent business people and can tell you anything they want. I think you'll be surprised at how open they are in most cases.

When you talk to some franchisees, you'll probably find some who do very well and some who are barely making it. Try to find out why some do better than others.

Remember the client validating the computer service franchise and discovered the franchise doing the best was a woman who had very little computer knowledge. She was actually *running* the business. She spent her time out selling and promoting her service and not doing the work herself. She followed the franchisor's business system and it worked.

This particular franchise opportunity might not be the right option for a computer expert who wanted to do the work personally. One option might be to hire someone to sell and promote the service. What role do you want in the business? Don't make the mistake of trying to do both, unless this is the business model recommended by the franchisor.

You don't have to have industry knowledge to operate a franchise if you follow the business system. As I mentioned, in my opinion next to divorce, failure to follow a business system is the number one reason for a franchisee to fail.

◆ ◆ ◆

After talking to franchisees, you may want to have your CPA look at the numbers. You may want to start looking for funding. Your CPA can also recommend what legal structure best fits your needs. We've discussed most of these options in the Legal Structure chapter.

Use your experts in their area of expertise only. You aren't looking for their opinion of the industry or business, nor do you need their emotional perceptions. Their emotional perceptions are probably worse than your own, and this is what we're trying to avoid.

You're now ready to start looking at where you're interested in locating your franchise. Until now, you didn't know enough to evaluate the market. The franchisor can and should be a big help in defining a market. We covered most of this in the Market Research chapter.

◆ ◆ ◆

Many franchises will ask you to come to a *Discovery Day* at their headquarters. This visit may be mandatory or optional. This trip will most likely be at your own expense.

The franchise may just want to show you the training and support you'll receive. You'll have an opportunity to meet some of the support staff. The franchisor may be evaluating you to determine if you'll be a good candidate to award a franchise.

Some franchisors invite every prospect to a discovery day. Some only invite prospects who are ready to buy the franchise. As I mentioned, I know of at least one franchisor who tells candidates that their discovery day is an approval process for awarding the franchise and expects the candidate to come with a checkbook and be ready to sign if approved. Some candidates are sent home without being awarded a franchise if the franchisor doesn't feel they're a good fit.

What every franchisor expects to accomplish with a discovery day is different. Ask them what they want to accomplish so you know what to expect before you attend. You don't need any surprises.

◆ ◆ ◆

If you think the franchise is a good fit for you at this point, you need to study the Uniform Franchise Offering Circular in more detail. Pay special attention to the actual agreement. Remember, it's a one-sided agreement designed to protect you *after* you are a franchisee.

You may now be ready for an attorney to look at the franchise agreement. You must have an attorney familiar with franchising. Having a family friend who is an attorney look at a franchise agreement is like having a plumber fix your car.

Unlike most buy-sell agreements, the franchise

agreement isn't negotiable except for a few things. For example, your franchise territory may be negotiable. Most things are not. Remember that the agreement is part of the UFOC and thus cannot be changed. A franchise attorney will know all this and won't waste your money attempting to rewrite the agreement.

A franchise agreement will define your territory in a variety of ways. If you have a franchise with a fixed location, or what I call a *Brick & Mortar* franchise, your agreement may say no other franchise can be located within "X" miles. Some states also have legislation controlling how close the same franchises can be located to each other. If the franchise isn't a fixed location type franchise, counties, towns, or zip codes may describe the franchise territory.

Your franchise attorney will be familiar with any state or federal legislation that affects your franchise agreement. Personally, I don't get overly concerned with contract points that are illegal and unenforceable by statute. State or federal statutes cannot be changed by contract. Obviously, it's in your best interests to maintain good working relationships with your franchisor and your neighboring franchisees, but know your rights.

◆ ◆ ◆

Now, and not before, you're ready to discuss what you're considering with your friends and relatives. They'll tell you what they think based on their perceptions and emotions. Obviously, they may not totally agree with your decisions. If they did, they would have done something like it themselves.

You're the one with the data and the facts. Discuss

it with them if you want, but their opinion is not relevant.

◆　◆　◆

A business that's perfect for one person may be totally wrong for another person. The business that's right for Sam would be totally wrong for Linn. The business that's right for Linn would be totally wrong for Sam. They have different personalities. They have different lifestyle goals. The role of each in the business is totally different.

Sam is the client I mentioned who was a very successful sales manager in the telecom industry. He made a lot of money, but he wasn't happy in his job. Sam was a natural salesman who loved to knock on doors, sell, and close deals. He had fun selling and it defined him. He found his job as a sales manager very frustrating. His sales people never lived up to his personal expectations.

One of the controversies in sales and management is whether a good sales person makes a good sales manager, or if a good sales manager is good at sales. I personally don't think being good at either one makes a person good at the other. Sam was an outstanding sales person, as well as a good sales manager, but he wasn't happy in the job of sales manager.

I asked Sam to look at a franchise where his primary role in the business system would be cold calling and making sales. When he heard the product, he responded with, "No way," but he trusted me enough to investigate the business system.

Sam decided the franchise indeed met his goals, talents, and resources. Unfortunately, Sam wasn't ready to quit his good paying job, and the franchise wouldn't award a franchise to someone who didn't work in the franchise full time.

I found another similar business model and system, but with a different product. This was a business opportunity and not a franchise. This business opportunity didn't require someone to start full-time which made Sam more comfortable.

When I presented the new business model to Sam, he again looked at the product or service and responded, "No way," but he investigated the opportunity anyway. After validation, Sam bought the business opportunity. He took a three-week vacation to attend training and start the business. He never went back to his telecom job. He was so happy with his role in his new business that he quit his job immediately.

◆ ◆ ◆

The Linn previously mentioned had a totally different personality. Though successful in her fraternal life insurance sales job because of hard work and tenacity, she hated her job.

After running some personality profiles, I couldn't believe Linn's success. She didn't have a personality that fit selling fraternal life insurance.

Linn and Sam had almost opposite personalities. She loved people, but didn't want to *sell* them anything. She liked people coming to her, not her calling on them. She liked more repeat contact with her customers.

We found a business model where her customer came to her and she could help them. The business had high repeat customers. Linn could get to know her customers.

Both Sam and Linn found a business in an industry with a product or service they never would have considered on their own. If you get nothing else from this book, I hope you learn to look at your role in a business, and not the product or service.

◆ ◆ ◆

I had a client come to me who'd been in management for municipal utilities. He wanted to start a restaurant because he said he loved to cook and entertain. He did understand that he needed a franchise, as he knew nothing about running a restaurant.

We defined his goals, talents, and resources. He soon realized his love of cooking and entertaining, and running a restaurant had very little in common. He validated business models that were not even food related.

◆ ◆ ◆

Don't assume you know where your investigation will take you. Keep an open mind.

I had a client we'll call Larry. Larry had a good job in the corporate world, but did not feel he had job security for a variety of reasons. Larry always thought he might want to be his own boss.

We started to validate. Larry's wife got involved, as she should. We looked at several business models and continued to refine their profile as they learned more about various business models. Larry's job turned out to be secure with a promotion. Larry decided to stay in his job.

Larry and his wife did decide to buy a franchise.

They actually were awarded a franchise for three locations that they would open over a period of time. Larry's wife and son would quit their jobs to run the business.

When I suggested they look at the specific model they finally ended up with, they said they didn't want anything to do with the product or service offered by the franchise. Luckily, they trusted me enough to investigate the business model. When they had the facts, they realized their previous perceptions weren't valid.

◆　◆　◆

Sometimes people look for a business investment they won't be involved with on a daily basis. The first thing people looking for are existing businesses like coin-operated laundries or car washes. Unfortunately, there are not many good existing businesses like this for sale. However, there are franchise opportunities available for individuals looking for a business investment where they won't be involved in the business on a regular basis.

In fact, I know of at least one franchise that won't even talk to a prospect who doesn't have a full time job. The franchisor with a business model for a passive owner doesn't want an owner with experience in the business. One franchisor told me, "We have a business system that works very well. We don't want the owner in the business on a daily basis messing it up."

This sounds weird at first, but for an individual who wants a more passive investment, it makes sense. The product or service isn't important.

◆　◆　◆

I once had a client looking for a passive investment. We found a business system that met his goals. However, we had one problem, his perceived self-image, and his perception of service offered by the franchise. He said, "I just can't go to the country club and tell my buddies I own that kind of business."

The product or service may not fit your perception for the business you want, but get over it. I once had a customer in the collector car business who was buying a 1956 Chevrolet Bel Air convertible in #2 condition for $30,000. Now it would be $60,000 or more.

In our conversation, I asked if he owned other collectible cars. He said yes, but this was a Christmas present for his brother. Since I considered $30,000 an expensive Christmas present for a brother, I asked John what he did for a living. He said he was in "grease and fat." He smiled, and walked away.

This really got me curious. Grease and fat didn't sound too romantic, and it certainly didn't sound like the type of business that would provide the means to give siblings $30,000 Christmas presents.

I did some checking. John was in fact in the grease and fat business. His trucks picked up grease and fat from restaurants, processed it, and sold it to the soap industry. At that time, he got paid to pick it up from the restaurants. Today, the restaurants sell their grease due to the bio fuel industry. Two plants then processed the grease and fat before being sold to the soap industry. John got paid on both ends. He provided a service to the restaurants and a raw material to the soap industry.

John had less than one hundred employees and

made between two and three million a year. Now that sounds a lot more interesting than just saying he was in "grease and fat." Don't get hung up on the product or service.

◆ ◆ ◆

I stopped into a franchise as a customer, and since I'm a consultant helping people find the right fit to meet their goals, I'm always interested in talking to the owner. The owner waited on me, and I asked about the business. He said the business was doing well.

When I asked him how he selected the business, he said it was an easy decision, because he'd been a manager for two franchise stores in two different towns. He knew his role in the business before being awarded the franchise. He knew exactly what he had to do to make the business successful. He knew what to expect for a return on investment.

This is a great way to validate a franchise, but may not be an option for you. The negative to working in and managing a franchise is that you may have to relocate; unless you can buy the franchise you're currently managing. You may have to move to where there's an open point. This option won't be available for most people.

◆ ◆ ◆

Retaining the service of a professional coach or consultant may be of assistance in recommending business models that fit your goals. I usually tell a client I'll get them someplace they'll probably never get on their own. I take a client outside their field of experience, and usually outside their comfort zone.

It's not that I have a crystal ball. I'm just profiling

my client and trying to match my client to a business system. When I present an option to my client for investigation, the reaction is not, "Oh wow. Why didn't I think of that?" It is normally more like, "Is he nuts?" I've only had one client say he ended up with an option that he might have found on his own.

You may be able to find the right option on your own, if you define your goals, resources, strengths, and weaknesses. You then define your role in the business and look for a model that fits. The most important thing is not to make the mistake of doing your initial screening based on your *perception* of the product or service.

Chapter 37: Return-On-Investment

Now, there's one more thing you must look at. Take a hard look at whether or not the business will provide the income or return on investment you need and want. I know you wanted to do that a long time ago, and maybe you did this as you were finding out if your role in the business model fit your personality.

I intentionally put this chapter last. It's too easy to get excited about a perception of demand and potential profits, and ignore all the other important considerations.

If you feel the business model is a good fit and fits your goals in many ways, it's easy to get overly excited with the opportunity. Now, you need to step back and look at the potential financial return with a critical eye. Is it too good to be true?

◆ ◆ ◆

I once bought a franchise that perfectly fit my personality, strengths, and goals at the time. I did enjoy my role in the business. The problem was that I didn't make any money. As close as I could determine, my franchise operation performed in the top 5% to 10% of all the franchises in the system, and I still didn't make any money.

Remember, just because it is a franchise doesn't mean there's any guarantee of success. If you're looking at a franchise, talk to as many franchisees as you need to be comfortable that the opportunity will provide you the income and return you want.

It's a little harder when buying an existing business. It's a lot harder with other opportunities, but do your best. It's your money you're investing and putting at risk. No one else can make this decision for you, or give you any guarantees.

◆ ◆ ◆

I once had an economic development director refer a woman to me. She was considering buying a small existing franchise. He felt uncomfortable with the woman's decision and asked me to talk to her. I reminded him that I cannot and will not make any recommendations on financial returns. He thought I might be of help anyway.

When I talked to the woman, she sounded very excited about the business. She had the financials for the last few years. The financials were approved standardized accounting recommended by the franchise and reliable.

The seller wanted $100,000 for the business. The business was just breaking even. The absentee owner paid a manager $20,000 per year. The manager worked about sixty hours a week.

I pointed out to the potential buyer that if the business continued at the current level of profitability, she'd just be buying herself a job. She'd be paying $100,000 for a sixty hour a week job that would pay her $20,000 per year.

I asked if she thought she could improve the business and if not, did a sixty-hour a week job paying $20,000 a year meet her goals. She decided the business didn't meet her financial goals.

◆ ◆ ◆

I have potential clients come to me who already have a franchise in mind. Often it's something they've seen while traveling or on vacation. They think the business looked like so much fun and they loved the product or service. The store looked busy and gave the *perception* that it made money.

I don't really understand how some of these franchises get to be so *hot*. Maybe prospective franchisees see a business that has a great image. The employees sell the hype and look like they're having a lot fun.

When a client mentions some of these *hot* franchises, I've been known to ask if they're just looking for a fun hobby that doesn't cost them too much, or something that can make money. As a coach, I know I shouldn't do that, and sometimes I just let the client validate the franchise for him or herself and learn what the potential return-on-investment is for them.

I once knew a person who owned five *hot* franchises in a metro market. These franchises were losing so much money that no business broker would even take the listings. This is sad. Eventually, these franchises just closed, and the owner had to take the loss. Such losses may not be limited to money already lost. There may be continuing franchise obligations and lease obligations that can't be terminated.

◆ ◆ ◆

Be careful. Now is the time to look at the potential financial returns with a critical eye. I recommend looking at three possible scenarios.

The *Best Case* scenario is what you hope happens and is normally not a problem. This doesn't happen in most cases and it doesn't happen overnight.

The *Most Likely Case* scenario is just that. It's what you can realistically expect the business to do. Does it meet your needs?

The *Worst Case* scenario is the one no one likes to consider. It's much more comfortable to just ignore this scenario. Don't. What happens with this scenario? How are any other investors affected? How does the legal structure of your business handle this scenario? How will it affect your future?

It would be nice if banks made business loans, so you could just walk away. Unfortunately, we know this isn't how it works.

◆ ◆ ◆

You're now ready to start. Don't procrastinate. Work the process. Don't skip steps. Remember, you're just gathering data and haven't made a decision for self-employment or a business investment yet.

You may go through the process and decide self-employment or a business investment isn't right for you. That's Okay. At least you'll know. You won't have regrets later and think you should have done something.

Have fun!

Terry Oliver Lee is a semi-retired business and franchise consultant.

He lives on Prairie Lake in Northwest Wisconsin with his significant other, Marla, a shelter dog named Skygge, and a cat named Poncho Cola Grande from the same shelter.

Terry Oliver Lee can be contacted on the web page:

BusinessFits.com

You may also interested in his Blog.

Common Sense, Business, and Politics

at TerryOliverLee.blogspot.com